DEZBA: *Woman of the Desert*

DEZBA

Woman of the Desert

By
GLADYS A. REICHARD

WITH PHOTOGRAPHS BY
LILIAN J. REICHARD
AND THE AUTHOR

J. J. Augustin Publisher New York

Manufactured in U. S. A.
The William Byrd Press, Inc.
Richmond, Virginia

Preface

THIS BOOK on the pastoral Navajo of the Southwest is the second of an Indian series. First Penthouse Dwellers of America which preceded it concerns the life of the pueblo Indians. The present volume aims to give a short account of Navajo behavior and attitudes toward their complex social and religious organization, a picture of daily life and adaptation to objects and notions which have been introduced by the Whites. It was written primarily to answer questions asked by laymen, teachers, writers, artists and tourists whom I have met during many years of sojourn with the Navajo Indians. The discriminating traveler who has wandered off the highway realizes that the desert supports a people attractive, colorful, even romantic. Yet his brief contacts with them may leave him with the impression that they are so reserved as to be stolid, so patient as to be shiftless, so mobile as to be irresponsible, so acquisitive as to be beggarly or grasping.

Such impressions may seem justified by casual acquaintance but I have learned through long residence with the Navajo that these Indians are, under circumstances which they understand, actually talkative and jolly; that, toward members of their own tribe to whom obligations are well-defined, they are faithful, tolerant, dependable and generous.

If the problems peculiar to the various characters are left with no clear-cut solution, it is because to date no such solution has presented itself. The Navajo have many difficulties due to the rigor of their environment, and to those troubles have been added the seventy-year attempt to adjust themselves to the ways of an alien civilization. The introduction of white culture has not been gentle or uniform in its methods and today there are many parts of it which the Navajo do not understand while at the same time many of them desire to embrace it.

Since 1933 there has come about a tremendous speeding-up of the transitional phase between old Navajo and modern white ways. The Navajo with their difficult problems and varied contacts demonstrate for a single locality a conclusion valid for all culture, namely that, regardless of major tendencies or drifts, apparently insignificant factors enter in and function so as to cause stupendous and unpredictable results.

In depicting the characters of the story I have used no incidents or details which are not true. Nevertheless, even though photographs aid in illustrating types, the description of the actors, the relationship they bear to one another, and the episodes in which they appear are all fictional. I know no Navajo exactly like anyone here portrayed.

For help in the preparation of this book I am deeply grateful to numerous persons who made suggestions and read the manuscript, and to many others who provided the means and coöperation necessary for taking the photographs. My greatest indebtedness is to my sister, Lilian, who not only furnished the photographs accredited to her, but also did all the work on mine.

February 1, 1939

G. A. R.

Contents

Illustrations

.... Navajo lounging outside .... *(p. 46)*

.... a cedar tree formed one of the supports of a shade .... *(p. 47)*

Silversmith's mother was as old as the earth itself. *(p. 54)*

She .... often washed out small pieces of clothing at the family washtub. *(p. 55)*

.... Alaba hauled wood .... *(p. 62)*

.... went along when they spread salt in the troughs for (the sheep). *(p. 62)*

.... her cousin who was now only nine and selling blankets of her own weaving. *(p. 62)*

.... the kingbird .... perched on the waterbag .... *(p. 63)*

Laced to the babyboard little harm could come to a baby .... *(p. 70)*

.... Little Policeman's father must hold one of them .... *(p. 70)*

There was no fussing if a year-old child picked up .... a pair of scissors .... *(p. 70)*

.... she was skilled in all her mother's arts. *(p. 71)*

Gray Girl .... always had a rug on her loom .... *(p. 78)*

.... the food-grinder was (a modern convenience). *(p. 78)*

.... had to haul every drop of water .... used .... *(p. 78)*

.... all varieties of horsegear .... hung neatly outside (the house). *(p. 79)*

.... he helped to haul load after load .... *(p. 86)*

.... laid it out to dry in huge piles .... *(p. 86)*

.... his horse which had become thin could feast. *(p. 86)*

When at sunset .... *(p. 87)*

.... she could hear the song of a rider coming up over the hill .... *(p. 94)*

.... and the sheep bleating toward the corral. *(p. 94)*

There must be .... a large amount of food to eat .... *(p. 94)*

Silversmith worked alone for many an hour. *(p. 95)*

X

ILLUSTRATIONS

Introduction

DEZBA is one of the 45,000 or 48,000 Navajo Indians who inhabit a vast territory in northeastern Arizona and northwestern New Mexico. Their habitat differs from that of their citylike pueblo neighbors only in being more versatile. The pueblo Indians, or Penthouse Dwellers, have adapted their lives to group living within a much restricted territory, whereas the Navajo have worked out for themselves group living in small, widely separated family groups spread over 25,000 square miles, which, with the increasing population and interest centered in a pastoral life, are constantly felt as inadequate to their requirements.

The Indians of Taos and Jemez have built their towns against imposing mountain backgrounds; those of Acoma and Hopi have sought as their homes high narrow mesas which project from the desertlike plateau in a spectacular fashion. The builders of the pueblos of Santa Clara, San Ildefonso, Isleta, and Zuni chose the lower places; their apartment-houselike dwellings are set comfortably on the plain near rivers upon which they depend for their water supply.

The connections of the pueblo people may be traced back to the early part of the Christian era and some of them have resided in their respective locations for a very long time. History relates them definitely to ancient peoples who seem to have been aboriginal in the Southwest, although each particular group has not necessarily lived in its present habitat since its beginning. The Navajo, on the other hand, are newcomers to the Southwest, not having been there longer than five hundred or six hundred years. All indications point to their migration from northwestern Canada where many tribes still live whose language the Navajo can understand in part. It is almost certain too that in the early days as they moved into the Southwest they attacked and destroyed some of the ancient pueblo people, or caused them to move from their original homes to other places with better defense.

The Navajo did not, however, take up their abode in cliff dwellings built in vast caves along canyon walls, even though they may have driven out the people who lived there, nor did they settle in towns or large population groups. From earliest times they seem to have been nomads, travelers interested in far places. The limitations of foot travel did not deter them, although their speed was naturally slow. The acquisition of the horse late in the sixteenth century gave impetus to their wanderings, and today the possibilities offered by the automobile for extended rambling are infinite. The Navajo who has traveled the continent from eastern to western ocean is considered enviable and informed. The myths of this people tell of gods and supernatural heroes who traveled, not only to the sky, but even "beyond the sky" on long or short rainbows, on zigzag or straight lightnings, and on hoops propelled by down feathers. Nowadays the aeroplane seems only a proper transference from a supernatural to a natural mode of conveyance which every Navajo who has the means will try, making him a traveler into space as well as in various directions on the earth's surface.

Since from the beginning the Navajo considered his roamings unrestricted, and because he moved and today moves all his possessions at a moment's notice to establish a new residence, he has not the extensive possessions of his pueblo neighbors such as permanent dwellings, pottery, and bulky, ceremonial materials. Circumstances provided him with stock;

the horse, cattle, sheep, and goats became a focus for his attention and he is able to move his choicest possessions on the hoof. In so doing he occupies a versatile terrain. The unobservant or uninstructed traveler may cover miles in the Navajo country thinking he is completely alone. He has not learned to discover the sand-covered abodes of the strange people who have spent some centuries adapting themselves to a desert and semi-desert environment, in making use of most of the facilities furnished by their Mother, the Earth, an animate vibrating personality who has their good at heart, who is lavish in color and atmosphere, and exacting, even cruel at times, about furnishing subsistence.

This earth takes the form of desert at places like Tuba City and Oraibi where rainfall is scarce and wind is fierce, piling up sand which buries such vegetation as struggles through to life. However, *plants do manage to survive* even though stunted in form, and, although life may be hard, the Navajo finds some means by which he also may come through successfully. The country rises somewhat as the traveler progresses east through Navajo country and, as sagebrush takes the place of rabbitbrush, huge rocks start up from the earth. *One of these has been named Steamboat* by the whites since it resembles a boat set at full steam moving out of the plain. Shiprock in the central part of the Reservation is a famous cathedral-like pile of dark lava with a splendid dike which projects from a dry desert flat.

In moving from west to east across the Reservation one crosses a desert with rocks almost alive, to gain mountain heights which in turn lead down to another desert, the Chinlee Valley, with rocks the colors of the painted desert as unmoving backdrops. Again a pine-bordered mountain road leads eastward to the "Fort Defiance uplift," *a vast expanse of country which includes the Haystacks and Window Rock*. Window Rock is a small natural bridge of red sandstone, quite typical of other such

XV

bridges which may be found sporadically in the Navajo country from the east across to the west in the region of Rainbow Bridge. The appropriately named Haystacks are only one form of peculiarly shaped red sandstone pillars common throughout the country. Only a few miles west of them Black Rock rears its imposing lava flutings, a shadow formation which points up and deepens the bright reds of the sandstone background.

Here also the desert vegetation within a very few miles gives place to that of the mountain. One rides through sagebrush with scattered clumps of pinyon and cedar, the hardy though often small tenants of the altitude of five thousand to sixty-five hundred feet, and on beyond as the altitude gradually rises to eighty-five hundred feet, to flat mountain places like parks where the tall yellow pine grows with no undergrowth, sometimes intermingled with Douglas fir or blue spruce, all in huge form.

Desertlike mesas, for at no place is the altitude less than four thousand feet, pinyonclad slopes, high mountains with tall trees and fresh flowers, deep canyons with springs and fertile alluvial deposits, all these are home to the Navajo Indian, and from them all he has learned to eke a living. Early in the nineteenth century he obtained sheep and goats from the Whites or Mexicans to whom they had been introduced by the Spaniards. In the summer *when the grass is plentiful they are pastured on the desert plains,* and it is not readily obvious how they find enough to live on. As the dry season waxes, the Navajo may move them nearer to the mountain. He may send them with a herder, for the family is interested in staying by its cornfields near the water courses where it raises corn, a good part of its staple food, for winter.

Luckiest is that family which has its range in between, in the scattered pinyon-cedar sections where sagebrush and grass are plentiful and through which run large or small arroyos which may be depended upon to furnish sufficient moisture to bring the corn to fruition. The characters of the story live in this favorable setting. Dezba's family has two permanent homes, one near the irrigation ditches fed by a reliable dam, one in the pinyons at an altitude of sixty-five hundred feet, surrounded by a wide and relatively dependable range. During the best seasons water is hauled for two miles, and during periods of drouth, the men may have to drive as far as six miles to fill their water barrels.

The change from hunting and food-gathering on a soil which offers small choice, to the agricultural-pastoral life of the present, interwoven with many adaptations from the other cultures to which the Navajo have been exposed, is almost incredible. Whereas in the old days uncertain supplies of deer, elk, antelope, and the small animals such as rabbit and prairiedog were the only source of meat, today the Navajo is essentially a meat-eater. He may derive fleshfood from his flocks of sheep and goats, although he depends on these for cash also. A few Navajo, where the Reservation is favorable, have some cattle which may upon occasion be eaten, but which are sold when possible. In spite of these resources few families indeed have as much meat as they need or want, and in extreme cases, resort to horseflesh for food.

It is possible that the Navajo took to raising corn very soon after securing the idea from the Pueblos into whose land he came, but during the migration and perhaps for years after, the women of the tribe, by dint of long and grueling labor, gathered sufficient wild seeds to furnish the family with cereals. Today they trade the flesh, wool, and hides of their numerous animals for wheat, baking powder, flour, coffee, sugar, and other products. Their main foods are meat, bread made of wheat flour, corn products of various sorts, and coffee. They like many foods of the white man, especially fruits, but use them mainly as somewhat rare treats, chiefly because they are too expensive for daily consumption.

All phases of life are a strange mixture of the old, often the very old, and the new. The metate on which corn is ground with back-breaking care may be found in the same home as the corn grinder through which the ground pulp or meal flows rapidly. With great pride men still wear skin garments—coats, breeches, gloves—when they can get them. The hat will be a felt sombrero, and the man's little child may have a dress of panned velvet.

The trees and plants of the region continue their old manifold functions. Locally some deposits of poor grade soft coal may be used, but *most Navajo use wood,* sometimes *hauling it for ten or fifteen miles.* As fuel, the so-called cedar, which is really a juniper, takes first rank. It is a small hardy tree which may attain a height of twenty feet in several hundred years. *Clumps of cedar grow close to pinyons* as if they were sheltered children, and at a distance or in subdued light look like dots upon the landscape. Cedar boughs are knotty and ragged with strips of bark, the gracefully placed leaves are flat and evergreen. The Navajo uses the bark, rumpled into soft shreds, to kindle his fire. Cedar wood is dry and splintery and burns with smokeless flame and sudden fierce heat, making hot lasting coals on which the cooking is done. Characteristic is the penetrating fragrance of cedar smoke, an odor which like that of sage, is incense which arouses a peculiarly nostalgic emotion in those acquainted with it.

Fire is second only to water in vital importance. A mother cooks her food on coals by the side of a small, well-controlled flame while her family sits around it to keep warm. At the oft-repeated curing ceremonies, often called "sings," which may last through the entire night, small family fires flare up against the dark, as somewhat apart, they surround the huge ceremonial fire of the Fire Dance, Night Chant, or War Dance.

For cooking, cedar is preferable since its flame is smokeless, but the pinyon is also a useful fuel. When there have been several days of rainy

xviii

weather, enough rain to wet all wood chopped or unchopped, the fire-maker finds the scars of a pinyon where pitch hangs in huge drops, sometimes hardened. This she uses for starting her fire, and the children like its pungent taste when they chew it as gum. The resinous character of the wood makes it ideal for large hot fires and the Navajo tolerates, even though he does not like, its black smoke.

Pinyon trees may be old and still be small, but in many places they attain considerable height, up to forty or fifty feet, though the name means "little pine." Unlike the straight neat yellow pine, they branch in irregular graceful plumes. Every three or four years, designated as "pinyon seasons," *the branches are topped by* green *pitch-covered cones* which turn to brown and drop their contents, appetizing nuts, on the ground beneath. The nuts are on an average a quarter of an inch long and an eighth broad and are covered by a shell which is easily cracked with the teeth. In favorable years as many as a hundred carloads of these tiny nuts may be shipped from Gallup, New Mexico, having been gathered by hand by the Indians in the vicinity. They are shipped to large cities where they are used in candy and as garnishes. This does not count the pinyon nuts consumed locally. The Indians have the accomplishment, attained also by some skilful Whites, of feeding handfuls of nuts into one side of the mouth, passing them through the teeth which crack them, and *allowing the shells to fall* rapidly *out of* the opposite side of *the mouth.* Thus they turn the mouth into a pinyon nut sheller, and in this manner consume large quantities of the nuts.

A third plant *of great value is the yucca,* one of the century plants. This is sometimes used among us in ornamental landscaping and is called the "Spanish bayonet." Two kinds are well known in the Navajo country, *yucca baccata,* or broad-leaved yucca, and *yucca angustifolia,* or narrow-leaved yucca. Both have thick fibrous roots, long spiny leaves, and bear a long spike topped by large, creamy bell-like flowers which develop into fleshy fruit. There is evidence even in early cliff ruins that the inhabitants used the root of the yucca for shampooing the hair, as the Navajo now do, and for this reason it is popularly called soapweed. The root of either kind may be used, but the narrow is preferred by Pueblo and Navajo alike, because that of the wide-leaved, although it produces the same result, makes the head itch unmercifully. The root is gathered by digging and may be used fresh or dried. It is pounded to separate the strong fibers, then soaked in water and beaten to make fluffy suds. It has a pleasing earthy odor.

There is no more satisfactory shampoo. The suds are as effective in cold hard water as they are in warm soft water. Usually the hair is rinsed after the shampoo, but rinsing is not necessary. The hair comes out of it with a glossy, soft, dry texture. Ceremonials of the Southwest prescribe the yucca shampoo as a part of purification for all participants. Navajo ceremonies require it during their progress and after they are over. Navajo of both sexes and all ages use it frequently also as an ordinary shampoo.

The swordlike leaves of the yucca have long fibers, which are tough and pliable. There is almost no limit to their usefulness. In early times materials for weaving baskets, sandals, headbands, and for twisting carrying straps and ropes were made from the yucca. Today the Navajo may get rope or string in trade, he spins it at a moment's notice from wool, or when butchering, twists a few strands of tail hair to tie a sausage. Nevertheless he remains aware of the utility of yucca fiber. Nowadays its use is largely ceremonial. The fibers of baskets used to be of yucca. Baskets are not used much secularly but have a prescribed place in ceremonies.

They are often called "wedding" baskets because one holds the ceremonial mush which the bride and groom eat alternatingly. The function of the basket in curing ceremonies is perhaps greater, but not as well

XX

known. When preparations for a ceremony are made, one of the questions asked is, "How many baskets must be provided?" They become consequently an important item of trade. Their manufacture is surrounded with such a number of taboos difficult to keep that Navajo rarely make them, preferring to trade them from their neighbors, the Ute and Paiute, who have not the prescribed taboos.

There are few ceremonies into which yucca in some form does not enter. Hoops are tied together with it and herbs are looped to them in meticulous fashion; headbands are made of it and worn by men who symbolically shoot away evil. Blades are set into sculptured mountains as a part of the symbolic sandpaintings used for curing. The whip which ceremonially initiates Navajo children in the famous Night Chant rite is made of so-called "yucca of the gods." Fresh leaves of the *yucca baccata* are roasted, the juice is squeezed out and used as a binder for painting on wood. The brushes with which the paints are applied are small lengths of the fiber with shredded ends.

The yuccas furnish food as well as fibers and ceremonial property. When the *yucca baccata* or *angustifolia* blooms, the flowerstalk and blossom furnish a delicious dish of greens. When ripe the fruit hangs like a bunch of small bananas at the top of the long stalk. From it the Navajo make several foods, treats rarer now than some of the choicest the white man furnishes them.

The fibrous roots of the yucca form a kind of ball from which spring the swordlike blades. This ball is cut and from it the ball used in the famous moccasin game is fashioned. When dry the blades are pulled, their points are cut off, and they are then used as counters in gambling. The pith of the flowerstalk is fine-grained. When dry it may be used as tinder when fire is kindled with the firedrill, nowadays only on ceremonial occasions.

The main reason yucca performs only a minor rôle in Navajo economy today is, not that its value from root to fruit is minimized, but that the plant itself is scarce. It used to be fairly common in many places until the cattle population became large. Now the stock devour it so avidly that few plants have a chance to reach maturity.

The cedar, pinyon and yucca are only three outstanding examples of natural products whose manifold uses, discovered in the past, continue into the present. Just as the Navajo uses these extensively, so he has learned many other facts about his environment, some utilitarian, some merely aesthetic or even entertaining. For instance, there is a tiny plant with a diameter of not more than six inches which grows close to the earth. It has a small yellow flower and a delightful musky perfume. Someone discovered that if this plant were rubbed on the side of a sandstone rock several feet in cross section, the odor would penetrate it so thoroughly that within twenty minutes it could be smelled on the opposite side, not faintly but distinctly. For this reason the flower is named "through-the-rock." It would be difficult to assign such a peculiar discovery to a motive stronger than play.

As he uses the products of the earth, so the Navajo also uses the earth itself. *His home, called hogan,* has a floor of earth, hardened by moistening and tramping. Its foundation is of pinyon or pine logs, carefully cut and laid one upon another. The chinks are filled with plaster made by wetting adobe. The roof is domed by overlaying the logs, and smaller sticks are laid at right angles to the logs. Over this foundation layers of cedar bark are placed and finally adobe plaster seals the whole so as to make a roof which will hold the heat and keep out the rain. If it dries and leaks at the first summer rains, it may be readily repaired by a new coat of mud.

If there is not room in the house for all his possessions, the Navajo digs a hole in the earth, lines it with cedar bark, makes supports to hold logs for a slanting roof, and, for protection, covers it with the earth he has dug out. He has then a storeroom with an equitable temperature, warm in winter, cool in summer. The moccasin-maker keeps his hide and sinews pliable by burying them in damp sand, as did the basketmaker of other days with the fibers she used.

The earth is a slow heat conductor, and once heated, retains the heat for a long time. Of this fact the Navajo makes use in the various forms of pit ovens. He designates a spot for one of them, keeps a steady fire burning over it for many hours, then digs it out, sometimes several feet deep, lines it with cornhusks, inserts food, corn, batter, and the like, and another cover of cornhusks to keep the food clean. Then he shovels on the warm sand and ashes, and continues the steady fire evenly over the whole. The time for heating is regulated by the depth of the firepit and the food emerges perfectly baked by the treatment.

As cedar, pinyon, yucca, and other products enter into ceremonials, similarly sand has numerous uses. One of the important methods of purification is the emetic. A bowl of sand holds the ejected contents. The sand may be gathered up with the evils which have been coughed up and removed without the slightest offense. Another form of purification is the yucca bath. The "one-sung-over" bathes from head to foot in the yucca suds which fill a ceremonial basket. He is careful to stand within the limits of a platform made of sand from the cornfield which has been carefully spread. On it special places are designated for the basket and for the patient's knees and hands, for he kneels to get his hair in the basket. The water which drains off of him must fall on the sand. When all is over, this may be gathered up like a blotter and the evils may be carried out and dissipated.

But it is in development of an astonishing art form that sand has taken

XXiii

a major ceremonial place. The pueblo Indian has his *kachinas* or representations of supernatural beings which require a large number of properties. As altars he uses also figures represented in sand but around them sets up many articles made of corn, stone, and wood which could be the possessions of only a sedentary people. Since the pueblo Indian has a permanent home, he has places in which he may keep these bulky objects and he may erect them in his ceremonial room called the *kiva*. The Navajo must have his ceremonial property, like his household goods and food, in such form that he can move it readily. His altar and his costumes must therefore be easy to fold up and indeed, the singer of even the greatest of the curing ceremonies, or chants as they are called, may carry all the things he needs for a nine-day performance with him on his wiry, rock-accustomed pinto.

Consequently, except for the properties contained in his skin medicine bundle which have become sacred through accumulation of ceremonial, age and use, the Navajo chanter makes the things he needs for each performance or has his assistants make them. Instead of *kachinas* with elaborate dress and painting, the Navajo symbolizes his gods elaborately in sand. Either he or his assistants have brought to the sing small sacks full of pigments, yellow, red, and white. They prepare these by grinding and mixing them with ordinary sand so they may fall easily through the fingers. They secure black by burning charcoal and grinding it fine; and the blue (gray), brown, and pink which they use, by mixing the original colors. The background is made of ordinary sand which may be dug near any home. Clean and of even consistency it must be when it is laid about four inches deep on the floor of the ceremonial hogan and smoothed with a weaving batten borrowed from the weaver of the patient's family.

The artists who assist the chanter may now begin their delicate work. When they are finished one may see a scene from the adventures or life of a

xxiv

mythological hero written in conventionalized lines, each of which has a meaning as fixed as writing. To each god is given the most elaborate accouterments: flint armor, feathered headdress, beaded pouch, embroidered skirt, arm tassels, turquoise earstrings and necklace, weapons; in short, all the symbols of his power and the honor accorded to him. The center of the sandpainting or some other part of it will designate the setting so that it may be clear to the informed that the scene takes place on a mountain, near a lake, or in an underground dwelling. All of these things and many more are depicted by the assistants, who sprinkle the dry colored sand through their fingers with practised skill to attain a complicated picture.

The casual onlooker sees a conventionalized picture without perspective, shown in soft earth colors with perfect balance, and can hardly fail to admire it even though he has not the slightest inkling of its meaning.

The Navajo who is being sung over sees in it the essence of supernatural power. He may not know the details of myth or of drawing, but he does know that it represents what has been laid down in the past as curative and what has been proved during the ages as helpful. The chanter knows what happened to the supernaturals in their wanderings, he knows how to make himself one of them, and further, he knows how to communicate this identity to the "one-sung-over." The patient has the sand rubbed upon him, from the feet and hands of the gods to his own feet and hands, from their heads to his own. Furthermore, he sits on one of the figures and by so doing absorbs its power. He becomes one of the gods. Since they were always restored when misfortune befell them, he also will be restored either from illness, evil or contamination, or he will attain the blessings of the god's restoration which will keep him from future harm. The interest of the Navajo in the painting, although having a strong element of aesthetic pride, is primarily religious.

XXV

These examples selected from a large number serve to illustrate the fact that the Navajo, although he may ride in automobile and aeroplane, though he may wear a Stetson hat and overalls, though he owns a victrola or a radio and reads *Esquire* as his favorite magazine, is nevertheless a child of the earth. In a country which to the newcomer is awful in its grandeur and terrifying in its demands of humans, the Navajo is at home. The sketches here given try to show him at home with his family, at home though abroad and alone, at home with conflicting obligations and attempting to find a place in which he may feel at home even though battered by notions from the outside which have small relation to his earth and which he does not yet fully understand.

Dezba: Woman of the Desert

1

Matron

DEZBA was the head of a large Navajo household. She was medium in height and stocky in build. The high cheekbones gave her face an appearance of strength which was further emphasized by the creases time had worn into the once smooth coppery skin. Even when her face became momentarily stern, lips, eyes and wrinkles indicated that firmness was accompanied by humor and that the mind was fair. Although Dezba was over sixty the grey hairs were few enough to be counted.

Dezba's family had many sheep. Every member from her older brother, Lassos-a-warrior, to her youngest grandchild, only seven months old, owned some of them, but they were tended in a single herd which Dezba managed. Every year they had to be dipped, for some of them had mange, called "scab" in the Navajo country. Sheep with scab do not fatten properly and cannot be sold in interstate commerce. Dezba, like the rest of her

3

people, depended upon selling her lambs for meat, and had to conform to the dipping requirements which prescribed at least one, and at times when the pest was exceptionally bad, two dippings a year.

Sheep dipping was an ordeal which all dreaded for it meant long drives for the herds to the place where it was held. Although it was well managed, the owner of each flock had to spend several days near the dip, and because so many animals came there, grass was scarce. The beasts became famished and tried to move away to forage for themselves, and this meant that they had to be watched more carefully than usual even at night. The family camps were near the dipping vat. Traffic of sheep, horseback riders, wagons and cars was continuous and the camps were dusty. The sulphur solution through which the animals were made to run was disagreeably yellow and had a disgusting odor. The sheep splashed it about violently and the wind blew it undiscriminatingly. Careful attention was required to keep the flocks of various owners separate and it was strenuous work to force the frightened sheep and goats into the liquid. Dipping was a task which required great patience, strength and skilful management.

Dezba was among the first to set up her camp on the bare plain at the side of a deep arroyo where the dip had been built. There were only a few trees and under a small one Dezba proceeded to unload her wagon and to make herself at home, as she did wherever she went. Most of her family were with her and all helped at the various tasks which came up. Before leaving to help another man, Dezba's husband, Silversmith, had unharnessed the team, and with the help of a boy had unloaded the full water barrel. Someone had put a saddle under the tree; it would make a comfortable place against which to rest. Little Policeman, Dezba's ten-year-old grandson, had brought his motherless calf which he had tethered to a wagonwheel. Gray Girl, Dezba's youngest daughter, who was fourteen, was the cook. She had brought her pots, pans and grill. Her butcherknife

4

was sharp and she was ready to prepare a meal. A sheep had been butchered, and flour, baking-powder and coffee were at hand.

Although dipping was hard work, it had its compensations, for Dezba's relatives and many of her friends were there with their families. It is customary for the daughters of a Navajo household to live near their mother, and their husbands work for their father. Two of Dezba's daughters lived with her, but Loco, the husband of the third, being very independent, felt that he could do better for himself than if he worked for Silversmith, Dezba's husband. With his wife he had established his own home not more than seven miles from her mother's. His wife, who was named "Alaba's mother" after her eldest child, had borne him four children. They were small, pretty, and impudent, the youngest of Dezba's grandchildren, and she was never quite reconciled to the fact that they did not live with her. *It was good to have babies about* the place and her home lacked them. Alaba's mother was too busy to visit her often, but she was at the dip and her children were all with her. Dezba could enjoy them to her heart's content for three days or longer, if for any reason there happened to be delay.

Sheep dipping was an activity which demanded coördinated strength. Besides her brother, Lassos-a-warrior, and her husband, Dezba's three sons-in-law and her son, Tuli, were to help her, as would all her female relatives. They formed a closely-knit group which would coöperate in dipping the flocks belonging to all of them as the turn came for each at the vat. Further, the group would help other families who lent their aid to Dezba in the same way, for dipping required much man-power. The three sons-in-law were in a particular class for they could not, like Tuli, Dezba's son, communicate with her directly, but had to learn her wishes through their wives, or through Silversmith, their father-in-law. This was because from time immemorial Navajo women have had the custom of avoiding

5

their sons-in-law. They must not "see" each other, although each always holds himself in readiness to help the other. The avoidance and helpfulness build up a special kind of respect which is incredibly effective, although the means by which this respect is established often create awkward and amusing situations. However, if any of her sons-in-law had failed to coöperate in the avoidance, or if one had been bold enough to address her or look at her, Dezba would not only have felt deeply hurt, but she would have feared that either she or her insulting son-in-law would become ill or even insane. Some of the young men who had gone to school thought the taboo nonsensical, but Dezba's sons-in-law had never rebelled against the custom.

In addition to the quiet satisfaction she enjoyed at the presence of her whole family, there was great pleasure in visiting. During the time they camped at the dip there were periods of exciting activity, but there were also intervals of waiting filled with sociability. Women from other camps would come to tell news and to enjoy gossip. They would help with the work which was going on. *One helped Gray Girl cut up meat* as they talked, and she was also on hand to eat the soup when it was ready. On another day, Gray Girl or Dezba might visit her camp, help her cook, and enjoy her hospitality in the same way. There were friends and relatives from long distances whom Dezba sometimes did not see for several years.

When she arrived there were not many people at the encampment, but they came in large numbers as the day advanced. Dezba had chosen to be among the first because her menfolk all had important engagements soon after. They had waited for two flocks to be dipped, and as the last animal of the second flock swam out of the dipping vat, Silversmith called all of Dezba's helpers together. There was nothing to indicate management, yet every person took up his place as if the act had been rehearsed, as indeed

6

. . . . plants do manage to survive. →

Photograph by L. J. R.

One of these has been named Steamboat . . . .

it had in thought and careful instructions previously given. Dezba had selected each helper according to his talents, always with the welfare of the sheep in mind.

Little Policeman, Tuli's son, who was only ten, was expert at driving the sheep and he was helped by other boys who were older. Through her husband Dezba had requested her three sons-in-law to take charge of the sheep at the corrals. At the gate just above the trough she had stationed her son, Tuli, who always won in contests of strength. The animals milled about in the runway, a mass of puzzled squirming wool. They came to the gate to find the only escape a short jump into the brownish water a few feet below. Here each stopped short on feet stubborn with fear, baahing with all the breath its fright left it. A few found themselves fighting the vile-smelling liquid before they could summon a bleat, but most had to be sent into it with force sufficient to overcome not only their natural strength, but also their paralyzing fear. Tuli was the man to win in the tussle.

Standing on both sides of the trough were young men who were firm but gentle, with them the women; in the midst of them Dezba took up her own position. Here she could keep an eye out in every direction to see that all went well, and, since the runway was at right angles to the trough, she would not see her sons-in-law.

The party, each one holding a long forked stick, stood ready for the run. A mess of newly-mixed sulphur solution had been let into the vat. The sun beat down on heads covered to keep the splashing "medicine" out of the carefully kept hair of the workers. No one wore good clothes. Velvet blouses and calico skirts, seersucker shirts and denim overalls were faded and patched, but silver bracelets and turquoise necklaces which indicated wealth were plentiful, for the sulphur could not spoil them. There was little wind and the still air was heavy with the smell of sheep, sulphur and

7

dust. The quiet joking and gentle laughter of the workers were a droning undercurrent to the frenzied bleating of the sheep.

And now the trough was full. Dezba's brother at the opposite end where he stood to count gave the word, Tuli released the gate, the sheep started in. The waiting workers sprang into businesslike activity, fast but steady. Here a goat tried to break away, was forced down in by a fork, there a lamb went under, was raised by the merciful stick. The big ram had come to the end and, shaking a bedraggled pelt, walked into the corral. In his eye was a look of wonder as to what it was all about, something of surprise at his survival, and a glint of superiority as he watched his unfortunate mates still struggling through. Shaking and puzzled, though vastly relieved, he moved away to make room for them as they leaped up from the trough.

For two hours the struggle continued, sheep and goats pouring into the runway, forced separately into the solution, and bleating in panic through the liquid, supported or ducked by the forks of the men and women along both sides of the vat, and finally attaining safety in the corral to which they sprang at the end. The dippers gave little cries as they became splashed unmercifully by the yellow liquid, and the women pulled their shawls of bleached floursacks closer to protect their hair. When the last of the flock had passed through, Dezba noted that not one animal had been endangered. The work seemed rough, and strength and force were required to accomplish it, but to be successful, gentleness and care at just the right time were required.

If the large animals swam through somewhat easily, keeping their heads out of the fluid, their heads had to be ducked with the forked stick, for if the scab remained on the head, it became the seat of infection for the whole body. There was a knack to submerging the animal and yet not allowing it to get sulphur in eyes or mouth. To do so might kill it. The lambs and

8

kids, on the other hand, must be supported, for the liquid was too deep for them. The skill necessary in handling all this had been sufficient, and it had not been applied accidentally. Dezba had chosen her allies so that those who were not rough, but were nevertheless firm and thorough, had stood with her along the sides of the vat. They had not had to rescue a single beast from the liquid for resuscitation, and as Dezba leaned on her stick she reflected with satisfaction, "None will even need help." Five had been thrown out of the flock which preceded hers and two of them looked as though they would die. Dezba thought of her friend who owned them, "She never manages well and her sons are rough."

Lassos-a-warrior had stood at the exit opposite a Government stockman. They were there to count the animals dipped. There were several reasons for this. One was that Dezba would pay the Government, by which the dip was run, a cent a head for the service. Furthermore, this happened in 1937, one of the years during which the Government authorities were doing all they could to induce the Navajo to reduce the size of their herds. In the last fifty years, well within the memory of man, the character of the Navajo terrain had noticeably changed. Where formerly there had been broad smooth plains covered with thick grass of which the best was grama or "buffalo" grass, the plains were now gutted by sharp gullies, some small, others large like the arroyo near which the sheepdip stood. Through them the water ran and cut away the soil whenever it rained, making the crevices always larger. The white people called this "soil erosion" and said it was due to overgrazing. They explained that the large number of sheep owned by the Navajo—and the goats were even more harmful—had eaten the grass so close that even the roots were destroyed. So short and sparse had they become that they no longer held the soil, and it became loose and easily washed or blown away. At first the Whites had strongly urged the Navajo to diminish their herds, and this year had required a pro-rated re-

9

duction, the number to be determined by the count taken at dipping time. Lassos-a-warrior had counted eight hundred ten in Dezba's flock and the stockman's figure checked with his.

With jokes of congratulation the various members of the family retired, the men to help others at the corrals, some of the women to visit other camps and to greet newcomers, Dezba to her own camp. Here Gray Girl had been assisted by Alaba's mother who had stayed behind to watch the children. Gray Girl had assembled her pots and pans around the glowing coals of her cedar fire. On some boiled a pot of goat stew to which corn had been added. Coffee pots filled with hot water stood ready for coffee at a moment's notice. Gray Girl had mixed a large pan full of dough thoroughly kneaded from flour and baking powder. She had patiently shaped tortillas by throwing small portions of the stiff dough from one hand to the other.

At her side a frying-pan stood on hot coals, and as she shaped one tortilla she watched another baking in the pan and turned it with a skilful flip. Just as it showed a nicely-browned center on each side, another was ready to take its place. She had a pile of six or seven as the family began to come back. Making a tablespoon of her left hand, she measured coffee from a paper sack into the coffee pots.

The women rested, fanning themselves with the floursacks which had protected their hair and catching their breath as they jested and talked. It was not long before some of the men came back and then Gray Girl laid a cloth on the ground. On it she set a large bowl of stewed meat in its corn-flavored broth. She stood large spoons on end, their bowls resting on the edge of the stewpot. She brought a pile of tin cups, a huge stack of tortillas, and a pot full of clear coffee. A jar of sugar stood in the center. Everyone there moved up and the meal began.

One pulled at a bone to which adhered too big a chunk of tough meat,

10

and Gray Girl handed him the sharp butcherknife. He cut off the size he wanted and handed bone and knife to his neighbor. Another pulled off a portion of tortilla, soaked it in the tasty broth, and scooped up corn kernels with it as with a spoon. Still another dipped up his broth with one of the spoons. Deliberately but satisfyingly they ate. As new diners appeared around the cloth, Gray Girl was ready with reinforcements.

As they placidly devoted themselves to food, a group of men approached. Some were white men who seemed excited and spoke in loud tones. The Navajo with them were just as excited, but they kept their voices low. Curly's son, Dezba's nephew who spoke English, was leading the party, and Little Policeman was with them, taking in all they said and saying nothing. Dezba casually continued combing the hair of a child. When she turned *she covered her mouth with her hand, her usual gesture of shyness,* as her nephew addressed her.

"This white man here says you have too many goats."

Of the eight hundred ten head dipped, one hundred four were goats.

"Tell him I have only a hundred twenty-five head and that is not too many," she answered, her expression not changing a bit.

"He says you had eight hundred ten when they counted just now, and the Government has made a rule that the flocks have to be reduced, so you have to give up eighty-one and twenty must be goats."

The stockmen hired by the Government in the department they called Soil Erosion Control were insistent that the number of goats should be reduced even more radically than the sheep, for they argued that goats ate the grass closer to the ground, sometimes so close that the roots could not survive. In addition they ate branches and bark of trees as high as they could reach, destroying many.

"Tell him they are not all mine," said Dezba. "They belong to many people. We just herd them and take care of them."

11

"Who are these people then?" asked the man.

"Some are hers," answered Curly's son; "some belong to her husband over there. Some are her brother's. He is over there too. Some are her daughter's, the lady with the baby. Some belong to her other daughter. She is not here. Some to that girl cooking there. This man here is her son. Some of them are his. He has a brother away at school and some are his. Some belong to my cousins. Some are Little Policeman's. That's the boy. And *some belong to my aunt and uncle.*"

The Navajo kin-terms were a handicap which the range men could never overcome. To Curly's son and all of Dezba's family the speech was clear, for they knew every person and every animal individually. But as the interpreter proceeded the stockman became more and more bewildered and, passing over the absentees, he finally said, "And where are your aunt and uncle?"

"There between the wagons playing with the calf. The calf is Little Policeman's."

When the stockman looked between the wagons all he could see were little children, the oldest at most five years old.

"What do you mean, your aunt and uncle?" asked the white man.

"That's what they are to me," explained Curly's son seriously. Whereupon the stockman threw up his hands, remarking to his assistant, "There is no way to understand their relationships. They just simply don't make sense. Guess we can't get at it this way," and they went off hoping they might find a way.

This stockman, like many of his fellows, was conscientious and he had made up his mind to do an honest job, but when he got to his twenty-year-old interpreter's five-year-old uncle, he was completely nonplussed. He had to deliver a specified number of sheep and goats when the reckoning came, and the only thing he could see to do was to demand ten per cent of

I 2

Dezba's eight hundred and ten head. This he did in what seemed to her family a high-handed manner, for eventually the family had to pro-rate the reduction among themselves. The rule was that flocks having less than fifty head should not be reduced. According to this ruling, only twenty-four should have been taken from this large flock, for Dezba and Silversmith were the only ones who exceeded the limit. The demand did not consider that the youngest baby of Alaba's mother owned only one lamb, or that the interpreter's "aunts" and "uncle" owned not more than five apiece. All this which was quite obvious to Dezba and her relatives was confusing and difficult to the officials, and they had neither the desire, the patience, nor the knowledge to follow it through. The result enkindled a dull resentment in the gentle minds of Dezba and her brother, which was fanned by the rest of the family as the discussion of the matter continued indefinitely.

When the stockman left and her men had left or fallen asleep, Dezba could not help reviewing the question in her mind. The rangers did not like goats. They said they ruined the range, but Dezba and her people liked them because they lived on less and coarser forage than the sheep, and because they were good leaders of the herd. The Whites despised the meat, for they said it was strong and tough. The Navajo did not find it too strong and thought one felt satisfied longer after a meal of tough meat. Although it was hard to spin, Dezba liked to use mohair for weaving. It was stronger for warp, and when used for weft, gave a soft outline to the pattern which was unusually attractive. Dezba would not have liked her flock to consist of goats only, but she found the small number she owned useful and profitable.

In her thoughts she turned from a consideration of the goat to the men who said they were trying to control soil erosion. The Navajo called erosion control "filling-the-arroyos-with-money," and there was something literal

13

in the way they used the word. The white people did things which seemed futile and expensive to the Navajo. Right near Dezba's place a dam had been built. Silversmith had urged its building and thought it would not be expensive because the natural rocks would aid greatly in its construction, and the trader who was a good friend of the family agreed. The recommendation was approved and after some months the dam was completed, but it was turned the wrong way.

When the Government had first instituted the Soil Erosion Control Service, the chief had told a large gathering of Navajo that they were going to plant small trees in the beds of arroyos to hold the waters when they came down. The interpreter had said this, but Dezba could not believe it, and asked some of her friends, Navajo and white, what he had really said. They had said the interpreter was right. She knew, as did anyone else who had seen a wash running, that nothing held the waters and that even large uprooted trees were hurled downstream carrying destruction with them. If the leaders did not know these things, how could she trust their judgment about the goats?

As Dezba mused the people left the food one by one. *Some of the men lay dozing under their big hats.* The women sat quietly resting, and Gray Girl, who never rested, washed the cups and knives and put away the surplus meat. They were all tired, for lack of grass had made the sheep restless the night before, and several times all hands had got out to herd them closer for they kept trying to break away. Even though their own sheep had been successfully dipped, Dezba's family would stay one night longer to help their friends in the morning.

Although there was much activity at the dip, there was a moment of tranquillity for Dezba. She could have rested, but since she had eaten she no longer felt tired. She had heard that the trader, her friend, whom the Navajo called "Always-in-a-hurry," was at the trading-post, which was

14

. . . . a vast expanse of country which includes the Haystacks. →

Photograph by L. J. R.

. . . . and Window Rock.

. . . . when the grass is plentiful they are pastured on the desert plains. →

. . . . *most Navajo use wood . . . . hauling it for ten or fifteen miles.*

only a mile from the sheepdip. There was a post nearer to her own home, but she chose to trade with him when possible. She was one of the best weavers of her tribe. Her weaving was firm, her designing sure, and there was no pattern too difficult for her to attempt. The trader told her what he wanted or gave her the pattern, and she usually had a large elaborate rug on her loom, weaving it at his order. Many weavers spent several years at one of the large tapestries with detailed design, but she had once woven a fourteen-foot square in a month. Today she had brought with her, not one of these, but one of modest size and of her own design.

She changed her faded brown velvet blouse for her new dark green one and slipped a new full yellow skirt over the old ones she wore for the dipping. She harnessed her team to the wagon, laid the rug, neatly wrapped in a floursack, on the seat beside her, and started her horses on their leisurely way.

As she drove up to the post she saw many horses standing at the hitching rack, many *Navajo lounging outside,* and, best of all, the car of Always-in-a-hurry in front of the gate. He must be at home. Deliberately she crawled down from her wagon. Looking neither to right nor to left, but seeing everything, even the new band on Many-waters' hat, she went into the store. Although it was one of the warmest days, she wore her bright Pendleton blanket drawn tightly about her shoulders, for she never went anywhere without it. As she stood motionless in front of the high counter, her distinguished face was somewhat stern in repose.

Modestly she stood, erect and observing, for many minutes not saying a word. During this time she learned from remarks made by the other Indians and by the clerks that her friend was in his office, that others were waiting to see him, and that, as usual, he would not stay at the post long. She knew he would see her; she needed only to wait and she was willing to do that. As she waited, never moving from the spot, a small reception got under way. Black Moustache who had lost his daughter last week came in. When his eyes became accustomed to the dimness of the store, he went over to Dezba and silently put out his hand. Hers met his in quiet heartfelt sympathy, tears rose, and neither said a word.

A young man, Warrior-cries-out, sauntered in. He was a blustering, smiling Navajo who could always make himself noticed. Now he did so by clanking his spurs on the floor and by rattling his flashy silver belt of which he was very proud. The others standing about smiled at him and he greeted them, "Greetings, my older brother," "How are you, my grandfather?" Then, seeing Black Moustache, he and the others left off their jesting cordiality. He advanced slowly with an understanding look in his eye, put out his hand, and for some time the two stood in a silence shared by all. When it was broken, Warrior-cries-out moved on only a few steps to Dezba, and now his spurs merely tinkled on the wooden floor, and a smile of calm, pleased surprise started at his mouth and was taken up by his eyes as he shook hands and said, "I am glad, my mother." He stopped by her and in low tones they talked.

Suddenly as with a strong refreshing wind, the office door opened and Always-in-a-hurry came out. No Navajo changed his posture, but all faces assumed an expression of expectancy.

"Give this man two bales of hay. Hello! John (shaking hands), go out and fix my tire, will you? Greetings, younger brother. How is it you are here, my grandfather?" Gently and more quietly to Black Moustache, "My older brother." Not pausing a moment, he greeted every one, missing none. Before he spoke to the younger men, he picked out Dezba, wrung her hand fervently, and, after a quiet greeting, turned a pleasant joke. He knew they had all been waiting for him. He would dispose of their troubles, but Dezba it was who followed him next into the office. The others could wait.

16

He leaned back in his chair, pushed his big hat to the side of his head, and lighted his pipe, inquiring about her sheep, the dip, her children. She not only answered his questions but volunteered information which he could use later. After some minutes of chitchat, she slowly drew a parcel from under her blanket. With appreciation he never expressed directly, he watched her unwrap it. Her hands, though delicate and graceful, were strong. They never blundered or faltered, never dropped anything, but were always aware of the limitations of physical force, always prepared to accede to those limitations. And when the floursack was unwound, a small blanket appeared.

The trader had seen hundreds of blankets, a few good, some bad, and many indifferent. This one made him gasp. It had the simplicity of great sophistication. Its colors were daring but perfectly achieved. The designs blended into one another in a soft, intriguing fashion. The trader recognized a blanket made of mohair yarn, yarn from the Angora goat despised of stockmen, dyed with the soft inimitable colors derived from Mother Earth herself, colors which had no exact formula, for Dezba had extracted them from plants she had gathered herself and fixed them with minerals she found near her home. The treatment of the dyes was of the simplest, but she had spared nothing of patient labor.

Many of the Navajo who came into the trader's office brought problems he could not solve and requests he could not grant. It was almost as difficult for him as for a Navajo to say "no" to a request. Dezba did not ask favors. She always fulfilled her contracts and her credit was good. Today she wanted to trade a little, but she wanted above all to get her husband's turquoise necklace out of pawn, and to that she applied the bulk of the sum the trader offered for the rug. It was a pleasure to watch her satisfaction as the smooth, brilliant stones glided through her fingers, then fell over her heavy queue as she let the necklace settle into place around her neck. Pull-

17

ing her blanket once more up to her chin, she went back into the store and her face gave no indication of the success of her talk with the trader. She bought some dyes for a new blanket, some coffee, sugar, peaches, candy for her grandchildren and tobacco for her husband. When she had finished trading, she lingered for some time.

The trader knew the store was full of people waiting for him, but he went out of the door of his office, bustled into the big hall of the house where some guests were talking, and invited them over to the blanketroom to see the new rug. They accompanied him eagerly. He threw it on the floor, and before they knew it they were kneeling on the floor feeling it, exclaiming over it, all talking at once. They wanted to see its creator, and the trader called Dezba who stood quietly by, understanding their appreciation, wondering at their noise, trying to answer, through her friend's interpreting, their questions, which sounded to her childish. They must never have herded sheep! How could there be people who do not spin? Who know nothing about knots, healds, or strings? Politely and monosyllabically she answered; the sternness of her face now meant slight condescension.

By the time she reached her camp again the sun was setting. Gray Girl was once more preparing food. The grandchildren clambered over Dezba for the peaches and candy. She had brought a watermelon too, and all, even the seven-months-old baby, got a piece of that. She had been lucky to find the trader home. She had all she needed for several weeks to come, and her husband would be able to wear his necklace of turquoise to the next "sing." He had smokes aplenty too, as the night settled down.

18

2

Dezba at Home

THE WEEK after the dipping was a busy one for Dezba at home. Here it was cool, clean, and pleasant, for Dezba's dome-shaped *hogan* was set in the midst of her range on the high well-wooded mesa. Her house, which was one of the four in the cluster, was the largest, for it was used as the ceremonial *hogan* when necessary. Dezba's brother, Lassos-a-warrior, was an important leader of curing ceremonies, often called "sings," and there were many occasions when one of them was held at her home. The ceremonies required a special house, preferably a large one, and Dezba lived in this one. When, for five or nine days, it was needed for religious purposes, she moved out and lived in one of the other *hogans* for the time. She considered it no inconvenience to do so, for the fact of having a "sing" in the house brought blessings and good fortune to it.

The house was a large one, built of logs covered with adobe plaster. As usual it faced the east and in front of it, where most of the household activities were carried on in summer, there was a broad space which seemed to be paved. Anyone who used water threw it just outside the door. It dried almost instantly in the blazing sun. The impact of suddenly thrown water and the constant tread of feet made the sand hard and firm. Every day one of the women swept it like a floor, and daily a larger area became smooth and hardened.

There was a smokehole east of the center of the *hogan,* under which an open fire could be made, but Dezba used a fine ivory enamel cookstove which had a warming oven. In the summer it was set outside where she sometimes used it for baking. More generally, however, cooking was done over the open fire not far from the house door. The fireplace was large, near it were several grills on which meat was broiled; the coffeepots, stew-pans, and skillets were all within reach of the fire. Under some trees there was a cupboard, and in it, out of reach of dogs, cats and goats, the flour, baking-powder, and coffee were kept. The trees furnished convenient spaces into which small objects were tucked and from which sacks, containing all manner of possessions, were hung. At a little distance *a cedar tree formed one of the supports of a shade* which served as a storage place for bulky objects. Wagon-wheels and other things which animals could not harm leaned against it at the bottom. Hay, corn and other food products dried on its roof safe from marauding goats. Horses were sometimes corraled under the shade. From one tree to another wires were strung on which surplus clothing, blankets and sheepskins were aired or stored. The *hogan* in summer was used chiefly for storage and sleeping.

About a quarter of a mile from the house in a hollow into which a wash led, there was a cornpatch of about an acre. The deep layer of sand here kept the precious water of melting snows and spring rains from rapid evaporation. In this seemingly unlikely spot the corn had been planted and, undiscouraged by the depth of the sand, the roots had pushed hopefully

20

until they found moisture. As the plants grew, the season became drier and, instead of growing to large stalks and leaves, they had thrust roots ever deeper and deeper. Now in the harvest season they stood short, stocky, and full of ears, and so deeply rooted that a strong man could not pull one out.

The Navajo, in contrast to their pueblo neighbors, are not considered farmers. The Pueblos spend the major portion of their time terracing, planting, carrying water, giving every plant personal attention. So casual are the Navajo about tilling their cornpatches, which often look like mere interruptions of the sagebrush, that most people, knowing them to be pastoral, have the notion that they do not farm at all. Almost every Navajo family has one or more cornpatches, and its summer home is determined by the garden. Generally they do not make a business of tilling but carry it on incidentally. During the whole summer at frequent intervals members of Dezba's family stole away from the house to work for an hour or two at planting, hoeing, or weeding. When her shoulders ached from long attention to her weaving Dezba found it restful to hoe. Lassos-a-warrior, after days of riding, revived his muscles and thoughts by half-a-day's labor in the garden. Even Little Policeman and Alaba took their turn at it, although they worked only for short periods of time. The odd hours spent in this manner provided in a good season a third of the family food supply.

Early in July when the corn grains were just beginning to form, the family enjoyed eating the most delicate corn-dish. The women picked the ears, pulled off only the outermost husks, and boiled the rest. The covering leaves had not yet become fibrous, the cob was soft and green, the grains were more of a promise than a reality. When boiled the corn was sweet, green, juicy, delectable, eaten somewhat like thick stalks of asparagus.

The pale green corn lasted for only a few days, for the grains soon matured and from that time on corn was available at all times and in many forms. The dipping occurred late in the season, and the early part of Sep-

21

tember found Dezba at home with a large number of women to help pre-
serve the corn for winter. To her great joy Loco's wife had come with her
four children. Dezba's two other daughters, whose houses were near hers,
were there, and Silversmith's mother, who was very old but still capable,
had come for one of her long visits. There were other women, too, who
were not close relatives but good friends of Dezba. It was common for
activities which required long-sustained effort to be done as bees. The
women divided off in various parties preparing the corn in different ways.

Gray Girl liked to work with her grandmother and they set about making "macaroons," a satisfying dainty which tasted different when fresh and
when dried for winter. They husked the corn, preserving carefully the
clean, light green husks which curled in even rows where they were laid
on a cloth. Patiently they cut off the milky grains until they had a big
dishpan full. Gray Girl then brought a sheepskin and laid it, woolly side
down, on the ground. On it she placed the metate or grinding stone. She
pulled her velvet sleeves halfway to her elbows, took her place kneeling
behind the stone, and started to mash the corn with the mano, or rubbing
stone. As she rubbed it over the slanting metate, the milky corn squashed
from it onto the sheepskin. With hands clever, delicate, and skilful as her
mother's, she gathered up the mushy stuff once more and mashed it again
until she had a panful of batter of a consistency like that for pancakes.

When some of the batter was ready, her grandmother came over with
the clothful of green husks. As she held one in her left hand she filled it
with the batter, then, turning down the top, fitted another husk over it,
turned down its tip on the opposite side, and laid it on a board. They kept
on working until the whole plank was covered with the confections. Before starting to cut the corn, they had built a fire which covered a space
about four feet in diameter. As they worked, one or the other occasionally
got up to put on more cedar wood, and by the time the plank had been

22

Clumps of cedar grow close to pinyons . . . . →

. . . . *the branches are topped by pitch-covered cones* . . . .

. . . . *allowing the shells to fall* . . . . *out of the mouth.* →

. . . . of great value is the yucca . . . .

covered with the cakes the wood had been reduced to glowing embers and the sand and ashes of the large fireplace were evenly hot. Both women raked the coals aside, dug down into the fireplace a few inches, shoveling the hot sand into a pile close by.

Then they laid the "ones-bent-over-at-the-tip," for that is what they called the corncakes, in radiating rows in the shallow pit. Grandma covered them with heavier cornhusks, then with the hot sand and coals, and finally Gray Girl laid small sticks evenly over the whole and left the fire to burn for about an hour. When the two uncovered it carefully so as not to get any sand in the food, the smell was an appetizing mixture of browned husks and the sweetness of green corn. The confections were solid like a corn macaroon, browned all over. Gray Girl gave some to the children, and the family ate them at meals. They were especially good for lunch for the herders because they were easy to carry and were very satisfying. Gray Girl and her grandmother had been making the cakes for many days and, as the surplus accumulated, had laid them on the roof of the shade to dry. When they were bone-dry they were stored in sacks for winter. When the wind whistled and the snow blew, the "ones-bent-over-at-the-tip" would be soaked in water, broth or goatsmilk and eaten.

It was a woman's day at Dezba's, but the men, before leaving for their respective pursuits, had seen to it that things were well prepared. Lassos-a-warrior had hauled a large pile of cedar wood. A short distance from the house Silversmith had dug a pit four feet deep and five in diameter. Some of the women had worked over the pit, heating it and arranging ripe green corn within it until it was even with the ground. Again they had shoveled hot sand over it, then coals, and over all they had kept a steady fire burning for a whole day. In the afternoon all the women came together, Gray Girl and grandma with them, all faces eager with curiosity and hope, for this was the exciting moment of pit baking. Sometimes the upper layers were

23

burnt, the lower ones raw. If the fire had been even during the whole time and had been continued long enough but not too long, the baking would be just right, the upper layers of food nicely browned, the lower sufficiently cooked. Only patient, regular attention during the day's firing, exacting judgment at the end could bring about this result. Many women helped at the arrangement of the pit-baking and at tending the fire, but they depended upon Dezba's judgment as to when it should be uncovered. As she helped shovel off the ashes and hot sand she knew that she had waited long enough, but not too long. The odor that reached her nostrils was that of corn thoroughly roasted but with no suspicion of burning.

The women now set about husking the ears as they cooled off sufficiently to be handled. Each child who could walk came up and got an ear and one was held to the mouth of the seven-month's-old baby for it to suck. The four-year-old who could not eat all of his left the remainder in the fork of a low pinyon tree until his interest in it returned. As the women husked, they occasionally ate. Little Policeman, riding in from the herd for a short rest, also got his share. Some days he had to roast several ears for himself, blowing up his own fire, but today they were plentiful and fresh. Bushels of this roasted corn would, like the ones-bent-over-at-the-tip, be dried and stored.

Among the women who had come to the working bee was Mary's mother, one of Dezba's friends who was poor and always in some kind of trouble. When the rest of the women were working near the cornpit, Dezba drew her into the *hogan* where she made a very small fire over which she parched ripe corn as her friend confided her troubles. As usual in telling her story, Mary's mother went back into years of history.

Her girl had gone to an Indian boarding-school from which she had graduated. Then she had had a job working as a domestic for a white family. For several years she had done well. She had kept at her work

24

steadily and her mistress was satisfied with her. She had come home to visit her mother occasionally and even brought a little money from time to time. Her visits were never long, and when she came she did not seem to fit in with her mother's surroundings. She had her hair waved, she used lipstick and rouge, she wore silk stockings. Her mother found these things disturbing, but she was immeasurably shocked when the girl wore slacks.

Then there had come a sudden change in Mary. She stopped visiting her mother, who heard that she sometimes stayed out all night. When her mistress remonstrated with her she became sulky and stubborn. Her mistress finally told her mother that Mary had got into bad company, a group of boys and girls whom no one respected. They worked only when they felt like it which was not often, they went to dances and got drunk. There was even a rumor that Ed, the charming young rake in whom Mary seemed most interested, was bootlegging liquor at the Navajo dances.

About four months before her mother took her troubles to Dezba, Mary had given up her job and had come home to stay. She was accustomed to sleeping on a soft bed, her mother had nothing but sheepskins. Mary had learned to eat salads, vegetables and fruits. Her mother was even too poor to have meat often, and many days had little more than bread, corn and coffee, or perhaps a few potatoes. The mother grieved to see her child so uncomfortable and miserable, but a wall of helpless silence had risen between them. Futility reached a climax when Mary went to the Government hospital and gave birth to twin boys.

"She has been home with them a week," confided Mary's mother to Dezba, at last coming to the reason for the review of Mary's life. "Now she is more cheerful. She likes her babies and works hard to keep them clean. She has gone back to wearing her Navajo clothes, for the wide skirt is more modest when she has to sit on the floor or the ground. But

25

those babies ought to have a father. The father of one of them is Ed Red House whose home is at Black Mountain, but since there are two there must be another man. I do not know who he is. Ed's father wants him to bring Mary and the children to his home to live. He says he will take care of them all. But Ed does not want to do that. He is having a good time near town and does not want to settle down. Mary cannot work now. If she could I would take care of the babies, but I can't afford to buy milk for them. Mary wants Ed·but does not want to live at his father's. I don't know what to do."

Dezba listened to the long worried recital with a sympathetic ear and periodically uttered short phrases to show she was paying attention. She knew only too well how poor her friend was. She was a good, but not industrious weaver; the daughter hardly knew how to weave. Mary's family had never had many sheep, they were always losing the few they had through some misfortune or other. Since they were not successful with their own sheep, they had not cared for the small flock which had belonged to Mary when she went to school. Dezba, like most other Navajo, saw to it that the flocks of her children when they were at school were tended as carefully as those of the children who stayed at home. When they came back they had something to depend on. A Navajo woman needed sheep and land on which to keep them, and she could weave. Mary lacked all of these facilities for she had given up the ways of her people, and her family, though not obviously shiftless, were nevertheless so unfortunate in all their undertakings that they had no resources.

Dezba thought over the matter carefully. After a long silence she said to Mary's mother: "If that man does not come back, have Mary come here to stay with me for a time. I can help her with her babies and she can help me. If, when they are older, she can get a job and that man does not settle down, I will keep them for her."

26

This offer was not wholly magnanimous on Dezba's part, for she wanted little babies about her home. Gray Girl would be overjoyed to have them, as would Dezba's two married daughters who had no living children. Mary's mother was somewhat comforted for Dezba's plan offered at least temporary relief from her aching poverty.

During the talk, which had lasted until it was nearly dark, Dezba could hear Gray Girl, helped by some of the women, preparing the evening meal outside not far from the door. The rest of the visitors had persisted at the corn-husking until the entire pit was emptied. All assembled around the cloth laid near enough to the fire so that they could see to eat, and feasted on meat, bread, coffee and corn. For a long time after they had finished eating they talked, and one by one the small children fell asleep. It had been a long day during which all had worked hard and accomplished much, and they went to bed early.

The visitors had brought their blankets with them. Dezba laid sheep-skins radiating around the sides of her *hogan* for those who had not brought their bedding, for some had come on horseback. Loco's wife had come in her wagon and had brought sheepskins for herself and her children. Her own she spread in the *hogan* of her elder sister and the two retired for a long confidential talk before going to sleep. Dezba's other daughter brought her bedding to her mother's *hogan* so as to be able to talk with the women sleeping there, leaving her own house, which was a log cabin, vacant. Gray Girl, Little Policeman and Loco's older children spread their sheepskins in it. There they played and chattered until midnight when they could no longer keep awake and Gray Girl covered them all up.

When the talk of the women in Dezba's *hogan* had subsided, she could not go to sleep at once. In thinking over Mary's story she began to worry anew about her own son who was at school. He still visited her

27

occasionally, but each time seemed to draw farther away from her. The white people whom he knew best seemed pleased with him, but one never knew when he might yield to the influence of bad company. Dezba was not going to let Gray Girl go to school. If she got into trouble of any kind, it would be at home where Dezba was aware of all that was happening. Here she would have a chance to retain her influence over this child. Besides unrelenting poverty which was chronic with Mary's mother, there was the uncertainty of strange, new ways to which Mary had become accustomed during her years away from home. A Reservation mother had no means to cope with white man's customs which led girls first to change dress and personal appearance. Next, children began to scorn social customs, and became fastidious about food and the Navajo custom of sleeping on the ground. At the worst, they took to drinking and became loose in morals.

As she lay, half waking, half sleeping, wholly disturbed, Dezba missed her husband. He would not be back for a week. It already seemed a long time since he had left. She knew he would approve her judgment. He would be as glad to have Mary and the babies as she, but she wished she could talk it over with him. As she drifted off she thought the sheep were jumping from the runway into the bakepit of roasted corn, and when she hastily pulled out one, a lamb, and laid it aside, it became a baby smiling at her from its lacings in its babyboard.

. . . .

Some of the women who had come to Dezba's for the "corn bee" stayed for several days. Visitors made themselves so much at home that they seemed to live there, but even when there was no company it was not easy for an outsider to determine the makeup of Dezba's household, for its personnel changed from time to time. The large *hogan* in which she dwelt with her husband was one of their two homes, and their favorite.

28

The other was ten miles away near fields watered by irrigation from a large dependable dam, where they planted alfalfa. Silversmith and his sons-in-law each had rights to use ten acres of this land around which they had built good fences. The men of the family had been working at the hay during the woman's party. Usually when the men were away from home the women gathered at Dezba's and, even though there were no visitors, carried on their work in little bees.

The exception to this rule was weaving. All of Dezba's female relatives were good weavers. They all wove elaborate rugs and once a rug was set up on a favorite loom the weaver did not move about with it, unless, of course, she was changing her residence, in which case she could roll it up to transport it. Of course those who were carding or spinning wool could bring their work to be with the weaver.

Living theoretically at Dezba's was Alaba, the oldest of Loco's children. It was difficult to say where she really lived, for she was with her aunts as much as she was with her grandmother. No outsider could have guessed who was the blood mother of any of the children at Dezba's, for, although each woman had a favorite child, that child was usually not her own, but rather her sister's or brother's. Little Policeman was a general favorite. He was the son of Tuli, Dezba's son, who was living with his mother for some time. Tuli's wife had tuberculosis, and since she was a "returned student," that is, had been to school for some years, she had been persuaded to go to one of the Government hospitals for treatment.

It was right, according to Navajo organization, that Tuli should return to his mother's home to live. Had he never married he would have considered his mother's home as his. The same would have been true had he been divorced or become a widower. Had his mother no longer been living, his sisters would consider their homes his, and had they not all lived as they did near their mother, he would choose his place of residence

29

among them. Since all but one of his sisters lived with his mother, there was no doubt what he should do when his wife went to the hospital. He brought his own and his wife's sheep to be cared for by Dezba. He participated in all the affairs of her range as if they were his own. He and Little Policeman considered Dezba's *hogan* their sleeping-place.

Silversmith's mother was as old as the earth itself. Had all things worked out in even balance, she would still have been the head of a household, with daughters, grandchildren and great-grandchildren living with her as a comfort in her old age. But she had met with many misfortunes which had left her without a home. Silversmith's father had deserted her and four small children. She had had several husbands subsequently and altogether had borne thirteen children. But in her day infant mortality was high and only three sons lived to maturity. Usually Navajo daughters bring their husbands to live near their mothers, sons go to live with their wives. Since Silversmith's mother's children were boys, she was left alone.

Silversmith's mother had never known prosperous years, years during which her living would be even relatively secure. Like Mary's mother, but for different reasons, she had felt lucky to be sure of food for a week, and consequently became a visitor rather than a dispenser of hospitality. In her old age she was one of the individuals to be pitied, although under the pity there was a tinge of blame or shame. For reasons which were quite understandable and doubtless unavoidable, she had missed the goal for which a Navajo woman strove, a home with progeny in large numbers to cheer her declining years.

For a number of years Silversmith's mother had lived alone except for a small granddaughter who stayed with her, and the two herded a pitifully small flock of sheep. Her nearest neighbors who were remote kin worried about her, visited her often, frequently took her and the little girl to their homes for a good meal. Finally the old woman became too feeble

30

The swordlike leaves of the yucca have long fibers . . . . →

His home called hogan . . . .

It was good to have babies about . . . . →

to be trusted alone, especially in the wintertime, and she thereupon took up temporary sojourn with each of her sons. She was most happy when it came time to visit Dezba, her favorite daughter-in-law. The old woman enjoyed the cheerful continuous activity of Dezba's home. She was able, even at her advanced age, to contribute largely to the work. When an animal was butchered she cleaned the internal organs and prepared them for use. During the ceremonies, she was expert at grinding meal on the metate for hours on end, or at preparing gruel which had to be made according to oldtime specifications which she alone knew exactingly. The visit which began for Silversmith's mother with the bee would extend far into the winter, and she, like Tuli and his son, had her sheepskin bedding in Dezba's *hogan*.

Lassos-a-warrior was Dezba's older brother. He had never married, had lived with his mother until her death, then had come to stay with Dezba, as Navajo custom decreed. His nature, much like Dezba's but if anything gentler, and his wisdom, made him popular in Navajo gatherings as well as at home. For this reason and because he was a singer he spent many nights away from home.

There was one other member of Dezba's household entitled to a bed in her *hogan* whenever he wanted to use it, although he spent only an occasional night or two there. Silversmith called this young man, whose name was Fred, his "son." He was really the child of a cousin of Silversmith, orphaned in early childhood. He had been passed about indifferently from one relative to another ever more remote, and only when he married a girl who lived near Silversmith had he come to the notice and aroused the interest of his "father."

Fred's was a trying case. He did not support his wife and two children. Silversmith would get work for him, reason with him and persuade him to take home some food. This the youth would do for a few days and then

← *One helped Gray Girl cut up meat . . . .*

be off again, perhaps not to be heard of for a month. When he returned, Dezba would speak to him and he would try again, but only to fail. When he came back once more, Dezba, Silversmith and Lassos-a-warrior treated him as if his good behavior had never lapsed and the whole cycle would be repeated.

Fred's advisers sympathized with him to a degree, for his wife was very difficult. She did not cook properly, she had two children who were sickly and under-nourished, she had no garden and did not weave. Time after time Fred left her; as often Dezba coaxed him to go back. Always Dezba's home was a haven for him, where he was not nagged, where he could expect a decent meal, where he could come to believe in himself. At last after his wife died he came to live at Dezba's permanently. When he could, he worked for wages. If he had no regular job, he helped Dezba's men on the range. Dezba showed him how to manage his money, tried to make him pay his debts, and occasionally succeeded in getting him to contribute a little to the support of his children who had been taken by their mother's sister. It was hard uphill work, but Fred had become much more steady than he had been when his wife lived. Without nagging or arousing his stubbornness, Silversmith, Dezba, and Lassos-a-warrior, with unremitting patience, had set themselves the task of making a respected Navajo of their unstable son.

Because she always comforted and never blamed, Dezba's family circle was large. The whole community respected her judgment and looked to her for help. Even if she could not make her aid tangible, those who came to her left with their courage and their hopes restored.

32

3

Grandchildren

ABOUT EIGHT O'CLOCK of a cloudless morning in October the members of Dezba's family were settling to their daily tasks. Dezba had started weaving at the loom in her *hogan* and was industriously thumping her weaving stick as the intricate pattern of her blanket grew miraculously under the clever manipulation of her fingers. Near her sat one of her daughters quietly spinning. Tom, the herdboy, had been sent on horseback to drive some lambs for delivery to the trading post where they had been sold.

Dezba had put Little Policeman in charge of the main herd and had told him to drive them to water which was pumped by a windmill two miles south of her home. That meant that the little boy was to herd within a short distance of home, for two miles was not considered far. He would drive the flock slowly toward the trough and, if a wind came up to pump water, he would hurry them. The boy planned to spend all

33

morning with the sheep between his home and the well. About noon he would bring them back watered so that they could be driven in any direction, even where there was no water, for two days longer.

Little Policeman was only ten, but he had often been left in charge of the sheep. Today he was saddling his horse which he called Yellow Mexican. The herder was small for his age and it was some trouble for him to get the heavy saddle on the horse, for he could hardly reach it, but somehow he managed. Alaba was watching him, for she was going along. Little Policeman would ride, she would follow the sheep on foot and find her own entertainment along the way. Just as the boy tightened the cinch, Alaba called to him. For only a second he looked away and felt the reins passing swiftly through his relaxed fingers. He looked back at once to see Yellow Mexican galloping across the sagebrush, saddle on back, head tossing, reins dragging.

Little Policeman started after the horse, but his legs were short, and Yellow Mexican, who was in a tantalizing mood, had a good start. When he saw his best speed was hopeless, Little Policeman tried guile. He ran around to head off the horse, but this maneuver was also a failure. No matter how hard Little Policeman exerted himself, the horse kept at least a quarter of a mile ahead of him. He finally had to give up the chase. It was bad enough to lose a horse, but when that horse carries off a saddle, it adds insult to injury. Overwhelmed by his lapse of responsibility, which he took very seriously, the tiny cowboy burst into tears. His large Stetson hat was far back on his head as he dug his grimy fists into his eyes. When the torrent of his sobbing had somewhat subsided, he turned back to the house.

He had a long walk, for in his efforts to catch the horse he had gone far in the direction opposite home. In vain Alaba had tried to keep up with him, and he met her on the way back. Crying with sympathy she

34

followed him. The two children came up to Dezba and Little Policeman sobbed out his story. Dezba was sorry for him, but laughed and said, "Go find Tom and get him to catch your horse. He came back for his lunch which he forgot, and he can't be far by this time."

Little Policeman went to find Tom. For some time Alaba waited for him to return but finally started off in the direction of the well by herself. Her cousin would catch up with her in time. She meant to model a little flock, a pastime in which she frequently engaged, especially when she went toward the water with the sheep. Not far from the water there was a bank of clay which was just right for fashioning sheep, goats, horses or dogs. When she arrived at the well, she washed her face and arms in the watering trough and filled a tin can she kept there. The clay she wanted to use was at the side of the road toward her house. As she went to it with the can of water, she saw the sheep coming over the hill. She continued her play and after a time Little Policeman drove the sheep up to water.

He had found Tom easily, Tom had rounded up the horse for him, and the day's program had continued as Dezba had planned it. After the sheep had drunk their fill, Little Policeman drove them onto the range off the road behind Alaba. When they were safe between Alaba and him, he tied his horse to a small tree and lay down on his stomach to watch a nest of fieldmice which he had discovered. The little mice had become so tame he could handle them, and every time he herded sheep in this direction he spent long quiet hours playing with the little wild things. Today he was glad to rest after the discouraging way in which his morning had started.

By the time Little Policeman had a carefree moment, Alaba had already prepared quite a herd of sheep from the clay. They were small and well-shaped. Some were ewes with sucking lambs. She had also made goats, kids and a dog. She meant to have the dog drive the flock into a corral. She had

35

just started to build the corral by laying small sticks one upon another when a cow with a week-old calf wandered along the road. The cow and calf belonged to Little Policeman, but Alaba paid little attention to them until suddenly a large truck drove swiftly past. Cars were not plentiful on this road, and they always fascinated the children. This time as Alaba watched the truck she was shocked to see the cow fall at the side of the road as the truck rushed on out of sight. Alaba went toward the cow which never moved again. Now thoroughly agitated, she cried out to Little Policeman who was so far from the road he could not see what had happened.

He started for the road, placidly at first. Then sensing that Alaba's excitement was unusual, he hurried. Speechless and helpless the two children gazed at the motionless cow for a time. Then Little Policeman, who had to watch the sheep, told Alaba to run back to tell their grandmother. She went off as fast as she could go, her full ruffled skirt billowing behind her. Little Policeman went back to his horse, and the sheep, understanding no need to hurry, browsed slowly over the hill whence they had come only a short time before.

As he had expected when he sent her, Alaba arrived home before Little Policeman. She was disappointed that no one but Gray Girl was there. One of Dezba's friends, who had a car, had invited her and her daughters to drive to the trading-post with her. There was nothing the three children could do but wait until someone came home.

Just before sunset Dezba returned and invited her friend in to supper which Gray Girl was preparing. The undercurrent of excitement was not detectable in the subdued talk with which the women learned of the tragedy which had befallen Little Policeman's property. Dezba, questioning, learned that the sheep had been driven into the corral for the night and that Little Policeman had roped the calf and led it into the horse

36

corral near the house. He had even tried to feed it, but it refused to eat hay. Gray Girl gave him some goatsmilk in a bottle for it, but it spurned that too.

Once more Tuli and Silversmith were working in the hayfields near the irrigation ditch and were staying at their *hogan* ten miles away. Dezba said they must be notified, and then the family ate supper. Tom, the herd-boy, was back with the horse by this time and Dezba was about to send a message with him when her friend who had the car volunteered to drive Dezba to her husband. No one ate more hurriedly than usual, and it was dark by the time the party, including Little Policeman, started.

The men at the *hogan* were surprised when a car drew up, but they came out slowly and for a time stood by the side of the car, wondering about the cause of the visit but not asking. For some seconds nothing was said, then in a quiet way the story was told. When the men heard the news they indicated no more agitation by word or gesture than the women displayed in telling it. After a long discussion they decided to visit the trader to ask him to phone the man who had charge of the trucks to see if Little Policeman could collect damages. They found the trader home. He phoned for them, but the truckman was not at home and nothing could be done. Little Policeman would have to wait until the man got back and took time to look into the matter. Meanwhile the trader advised, "Better get busy and make jerky out of it."

Little Policeman had had a long hard day, and his father bought him a nickel's worth of candy.

Tuli went with the women and his son when Dezba's friend drove them home. They went to the scene of the accident where Tuli examined all clues carefully. From the condition of the cow and the position in which it was lying he concluded that the truck, going fast, had hit it, knocked it down, and killed it instantly. He also said the truck which was

37

responsible would have a dent at a particular point in the front. Then after all decided there was nothing anyone could do that night, the friend drove the family home.

The next day everyone helped at butchering the cow. When the meat was brought home it was cut into thin strips which were hung out on all available wire lines to dry. Dried meat in this form is called "jerky," and now that the weather was cool would keep well until the family could use it all.

It was only fair that Little Policeman should be reimbursed by the truck owner for the loss of his cow, reasoned Dezba and Tuli. It did not occur to them to note that the cow had been standing in the road, for this, their range, was open and unfenced. Even though there was no doubt in their minds that the boy should be paid, they had no assurance that he could collect. A cow furnishes a great deal of meat. It would be unthinkable to waste it, consequently they would use as much of it as they could. If Little Policeman could not collect, the cow would not be a total loss. If the truck owner did not pay him, the family would nevertheless have meat for days to come.

. . . .

Alaba's life was not much restricted. If she felt like it, she rose early in the morning after her elders had started their tasks. If she did not, she could sleep until she was ready to rub the sleep from her eyes. Sometimes she washed her face and hands, but usually she did not. *She* liked water and *often washed out small pieces of clothing at the family washtub*. She always dabbled, splashed and slopped in the watering-trough when she went there, but she had no habitual time for ablutions. When Dezba or Gray Girl or one of the other women thought of it, they told her to wash and occasionally inspected her neck and ears, but not often enough to make cleanliness a burden. At irregular intervals when she thought of it

38

The party, each one holding a long forked stick, stood ready for the run. →

Dezba would have a child fetch the old-fashioned hairbrush made of wild broom, and then she *would brush down the unruly hair,* forcing it into a queue like her own smooth shapely one. Alaba's hair was not yet long and flowing like that of her cousin, but her elders brushed it back into a knot.

The family usually ate three times a day. All ate before separating for the day's work. Those who were home might eat at noon, and at night, often long after dark, the whole group once more assembled for a meal. If she felt like it, Alaba ate with them. More generally she walked about eating a tortilla or sucking on a bone, avoiding regularity as much as possible. If she sat with the others to eat, it was because she wanted to listen to what they had to say.

As soon as she was up, she pursued her own affairs, which were in many ways an exact duplicate of the activities of her elders. Dezba made her put on shoes when she got up, but as soon as she went out of her grandmother's sight she took them off and hung them in a tree until she should return, and then she sometimes forgot them and arrived home barefoot. When this happened her grandmother scolded her sufficiently to keep the shoes from being lost; never was her chiding severe. All the plants of the range were rough and there were many small clumps of cactus, but Alaba had learned to walk so unerringly amongst them that she seldom got a thorn in her foot.

As she accompanied Little Policeman or Tom when they herded the sheep near home, so she also *went along when they spread salt in the troughs for* them. She liked to swing the rattle, a tin can bent to hold three pebbles, which she used to drive the sheep together.

One or the other of the *hogans* always had a litter of kittens or puppies which Alaba and Little Policeman wore out with mauling. At best the pets were not plump, for they had to live on what they could snatch when

39

— .... *she covered her mouth with her hand, her usual gesture of shyness* ....

the family ate. Most bones were cleaned white by the strong teeth of the people before the animals had a chance at them. If the children became rough with the dogs or cats, they were never called off or reprimanded by their elders, who believed that if a useless animal could not defend itself it deserved no protection. Besides they wanted their children to have a good time. The attitude toward lambs and kids was different, and they were protected and fed, even artificially when necessary, because they were useful.

Little Policeman had a little wagon. When he or *Alaba hauled wood* in it they paid special attention to the intricate patterns the wheels made in the sand, just as they enjoyed the designs made by the soles of their new shoes.

Alaba was a herdgirl by temperament, and by the time she was six she had not yet become a slave to the fascination of towcards, spindles, batten and loom as had *her cousin who was now only nine and selling blankets of her own weaving*. Dezba often said to her friends, and there was a faint note of shame in her voice, "She can't weave. She never tries to spin. She always runs away with the sheep."

Only by her tone did Dezba indicate her disappointment, never did she force the child, but she secretly feared her favorite granddaughter would grow up to be like one of her cousins who could hardly stay at home with her young baby, so anxious was she to be out wandering over the hills.

Although Alaba found many things of interest at home, the possibilities for entertainment when herding were even more numerous. When she did not play with mud and clay, she watched Little Policeman's mice, called his because he had found them. For hours she felt their soft fuzz in her cupped palm or watched their funny little noses twitch. Too high to be disturbed by the children, but easy to see with their sharp eyes, was a bluebird's nest. The children noted every habit of the busy parents, from

40

the time the nest was started until all the little ones had flown away, when they missed them for a time but were soon diverted by other things.

When they tired of mice and birds or when the season for them was over, the children spent endless hours watching the ants. These were very different from kittens, puppies and lambs, for they protected themselves by their fierce bite. Indeed, if Dezba wanted Alaba to go away from some place where she persisted in staying, she would only have to say, "You are sitting on an ant," and the child moved as if she had been stuck with a pin.

Some of the anthills were large. On them were pretty stones which the ants had brought up from their subterranean rooms. One day Alaba found a bit of turquoise, gleaming blue, on one of the hills. Frequently she saw a contest between the ants and a beetle and she often followed the beetle track to its source.

By constant practise the children had become so adept at catching swift-moving animals that even Alaba rarely missed. They caught the blue lizard which darted over the roots of trees. At one place to which they drove the sheep there was a village of prairiedogs, rodents with thick, fat bodies and disproportionately small heads, which scampered madly for their holes when frightened. When they could leap to safety in a second's time, they stood up on their hind legs and looked about curiously.

Alaba and her cousin often hunted prairiedogs. Each sat by a hole which by its appearance showed habitation, and, with eyes glued to the spot and without moving a muscle for many minutes, waited for a prairie-dog to emerge. When it did, a sweep of the hand, sudden but so smooth as to be indiscernible, caught the animal and choked it. A prairiedog is a small tidbit for a large family where all share. Alaba and Little Police-man almost never took their quarry home, but were more likely to build a fire, bury the little animal in the hot sand, and eat it after it was thoroughly cooked.

41

One day Alaba had heard her grandmother and her aunt discussing the imminence of the birth of another aunt's baby. Alaba could not make out when the baby was to come, but she had heard Gray Girl say the baby was to be hers. Like Dezba, Gray Girl and Alaba felt that the family needed a baby. Alaba was the youngest child in the large family, and she, being six, though small for her age, was by no means a baby, but rather, a big girl. After hearing the hopeful conversation and sensing Gray Girl's anticipation, Alaba could not get the idea of a baby out of her mind. It was so strong that it made her restless and dissatisfied with all her usual entertainment. For long minutes she sat and dreamed, doing nothing at all. She even failed to notice *the kingbird* which *perched on the waterbag* Little Policeman's father had left hanging on a tree.

It never occurred to Alaba that if she had lived at home with her mother she would constantly have had a baby to play with, for Alaba was the oldest of the four children and the youngest was only seven months old. Perhaps she did not even realize that she was more closely related to her brothers and sisters than she was to Little Policeman, for when she was less than a year old her mother had "given" Alaba to Dezba. Navajo women sometimes give a child to a mother or sister, and after that it is considered and always referred to as the child of the recipient.

The day the little girl became obsessed with the need for a baby, the hours lagged and as the morning lengthened slowly she urged Little Policeman to drive the sheep home. When the grass was plentiful, as it was after the rains, the children drove the sheep home at noon and ate there instead of taking their lunch with them. This day when Alaba coaxed Little Policeman to start home early, he only laughed at her and said it was not nearly time to go. She waited for what seemed to her interminable hours and then started off ahead of the flock.

When she arrived home everyone was in Dezba's *hogan* grouped around

42

Mary who had come with her twins. Alaba was speechless and almost motionless with surprise and pleasure. Passionately as she had longed for a baby, never had she dreamed of two exactly alike. Now her restlessness disappeared and she quietly squeezed herself into a seat between Dezba who was holding one of the infants and Gray Girl who had the other, while Mary and Alaba's aunts looked on and admired. Alaba could not believe the children were both real, and once in a while she reached over and laid her hand lightly on the cheek of one baby and then the other to prove to herself her eyes were not playing tricks on her.

She then began to recall a story her "grandfather," Lassos-a-warrior, had told them on winter nights, a story to which she had listened many times between waking and sleeping. It was the tale of the War Gods which were said to be twin children of the Sun and Earth Mother. Because they had the most wonderful parents in the world, they were endowed with all the powers of earth and heaven. Even as newborn babies the cradleboards in which they were laced showed the supernatural gifts and predicted the extraordinary career of the two children.

The myth had it that they were born in winter, and that one had been bathed in ice, the other in snow. This severe treatment had made them strong and healthy from the very moment of their birth. Gods who had acted as midwives to their mother gave each child a marvelous cradleboard, shaped just like those in which Navajo children are carried to this day. The cradleboard of the elder child had the name Dark Water. The two boards which formed its foundation were made of the Sun's turquoise earstrings. The bowed board at the top over the baby's face was a rainbow. When the cradle was ready, the baby was laid on a mirage pillow and covered with blankets of darkness, dawn, blue-rising-from-the-east-at-sunset, yellow-evening-light, and mirage. The child under these was tied in with side lacings of zigzag lightning. These were caught by a loose

43

central string of the same substance, and over all sunrays were thrown. The cradle of the younger twin was not very different, except in the position of the colors, and the strings which were of heat lightning. Its name was Blue Water.

As she looked at Mary's twins, Alaba thought of the wonderful First Twins. Mary's were boys too. They had no cradleboards. They were wrapped tightly in blue "bunny" blankets which Mary's former mistress had given her. Alaba could only marvel at them, but when her first surprise had somewhat cooled, her fingers itched to undress them so she could dress them again. Mary would not let her do that now for they were going to sleep.

Even though the babies slept a long time, not much work was done that afternoon, and for the first time Alaba did not want to help Little Policeman with the sheep. He would rather have stayed home himself and only reluctantly, after Dezba's voice became firmer than usual, did he start off. When the babies woke, Alaba could only watch them, for Dezba and Gray Girl not only needed them as much as Alaba, but they were older and stronger and simply took possession. Alaba could see the tiny round balls that did for toes, and she made the infants wrinkle their funny flat noses as they squinted at her. She tried her best to make them laugh because the person who makes a baby laugh aloud the first time must give it a present, and every member of the family would like to have that honor.

When the men came home Alaba's chances to hold a baby were even slimmer, for *Little Policeman's father must hold one of them* even while he ate. When Gray Girl had to give up the other in order to serve the meal, the herdboy took it and kept it until it slept.

During all the fussing over her babies Mary almost beamed. Here they were wanted, she was forgotten, and no one thought of disgrace. When

44

she was at home she always looked glum, she moved with dragging feet and answered her mother's nagging in monosyllables. Dezba's family displayed no sense of blame. When Tuli said he thought the infants should have cradleboards and he would make some tomorrow, Mary was glad it was dark for she almost wept for joy. At the hospital nurses and doctor had told her how to care for the children, and she followed their instructions as well as she could. They had not of course recommended keeping them in the usual Navajo baby-carriers, but Mary knew that they would be safer for the children in the surroundings of a *hogan*. There was no other safe place in which they could sleep. The other children, even though like Alaba they were really not large or strong enough, insisted upon carrying the babies about. *Laced to the babyboard little harm could come to a baby,* even if a small child were unfortunate enough to drop it or knock it over.

Usually the father or the uncle of a child makes its cradleboard. If he is old-fashioned in his belief he gathers the materials ritualistically, putting himself to no end of trouble to follow the prescriptions laid down in mythological times to imitate the cradles of the Holy Twins. These twins were not born into an orthodox family. They had no father. Not only were their uncles ignorant of the way in which even ordinary cradleboards were made, but none of them stuck to an exacting task like this long enough to finish it. And now Tuli had offered to do this. Mary's heart nearly burst with gratitude at the kindness of this household, but her face, although no longer as heavy as usual, retained its immobile expression. Tuli would not be sorry. She would never forget this. A time would come when she could do something for him, and then he should be thanked.

45

. . . . some belong to my aunt and uncle.

Photograph by L. J. R.

Some of the men lay dozing under their big hats.

Photograph by L. J. R.

. . . . Navajo lounging outside . . . .

. . . . *a cedar tree formed one of the supports of a shade* . . . .

4

Her Mother's Daughter

TO DEZBA, as to other Navajo women, bringing up children was a simple, casual matter, a procedure well understood which one treated as one did sheep-raising or weaving in a matter-of-fact way. From the time a baby was born it was considered an individual. Property in the form of stock was set aside for it, and when there was increase, ownership was carefully marked by a new brand. As soon after its birth as the child's mother could attend ceremonies, she took it with her and every ritual act was performed for it as seriously as for the adults present. If ashes were blown from a feather to drive off evil things, a feather was laid on the baby and its mother or the women sitting nearest blew off the ashes for it. If the prayer of blessing was made, some of the pollen which carried the prayer was placed at the baby's mouth and on its head, and a little was thrown up into the air, so that it, like the others in the *hogan,* might go its way with blessing. A baby was just as much a person as its father. It was for a time, a short time only, helpless, and things had to be done for it, but there was no delay in the time it took to learn to take care of itself.

There was no fussing if a year-old child picked up a butcherknife or *a pair of scissors,* nor was it snatched out of the baby's hands. By its own experience it learned that sharp pointed objects cut and stick, and in the same way the child learned to control such objects. As long as a baby kept well the system worked, but the incipience of illness was hardly noticed. When suddenly a child became violently ill, as they often did, the best a mother could do was to pet it and try to stop its crying.

Dezba had lost two children in early infancy, but with her living children had been unusually fortunate. Their illnesses had been slight and they had matured normally. They all had faults which were not too difficult to correct. One daughter was lazy but had a disarming way of getting others to do things for her. One son was stubborn but Dezba and Lassos-a-warrior had learned how to persuade him to do things he had set himself against. In Gray Girl's development there had not been even such minor difficulties. She had never been ill. From earliest childhood she had been unusually active, and merely seeing an adult do something like making fire or spinning yarn inspired her to try to do it too. She was allowed to try anything she wanted to do, and by the time she was ten *she was skilled in all her mother's arts.* In weaving at the age of five she had set a precedent of which Dezba was unduly proud. Although she did not say much about it, she glowed with pleasure when others remarked upon it.

By the time *Gray Girl* was ten she *always had a rug on her loom* just as her mother and other expert weavers had. She had even woven a saddle-blanket for her father. It was made according to old-fashioned methods which only a few women now understand. When she was eight, Gray Girl had learned to sew on her mother's sewing-machine which was one

48

of her most useful implements. Now when she was fourteen the family depended on her to stitch the women's velvet blouses and full beruffled skirts as well as the gay red and yellow shirts the men wore to races and social gatherings. Indeed, it was not unusual for Gray Girl to take prizes in exhibits which were frequently held on the Reservation.

When Dezba thought over the matter, she could not remember having taught her daughter to cook, and yet Gray Girl, when not assigned to herding, prepared most of the family's food and did a large proportion of the other housework. One reason she did this was because she always started a task while the other women were thinking of starting. They, seeing Gray Girl at it, knew it would be done properly. It was unnecessary for them to bestir themselves.

Dezba did not recognize Gray Girl's energy as a reflection of her own, for in her youth she had behaved in the same way. When Dezba considered with thankfulness the talents of her youngest child, she thought of the vitality of her own mother, who at sixty was the first one up in the morning and indicated her wakefulness by thumping her ax at the woodpile to the shame of the younger sleepyheads.

Nowadays the Navajo had many shortcuts to labor such as they did not have in Dezba's youth. The sewing-machine was one and *the food-grinder was* another. The family had had a grinder for only a few years and Gray Girl, like her mother, had learned to grind corn on the old-fashioned metate, a sloping stone over which a smaller stone was rubbed with back-breaking patience, really a handmill.

From long practise Gray Girl's back and arms were strong and she could keep at hand-grinding for a long time. Now that she was a little more than fourteen, both she and her mother had occasion to be glad for her strength and endurance. Gray Girl had become a woman as was evidenced by the appearance of her first menses. This was a crisis which had

49

to be handled with great care and attention, for it was believed that everything Gray Girl did during the first four days of this period would determine her future.

During her whole life she had had instructions about this important time of her career, but now Lassos-a-warrior, the repository of learning, gave a review of details which he did not want Gray Girl or the women who had her in charge to forget. She should not sleep much, and during the brief hours when she did sleep she should lie on her back. She should not eat meat or anything with seasoning during these four days. Sweets and sweetening were especially forbidden. Her diet should be corn foods with no salt added. She should drink very little water and that should not touch her lips, but pass through a tube through which she should drink. She should not scratch her head or her body with her nails. To do so would leave scars wherever her nails touched. All of these requirements were to prevent her from being ugly. If she kept them, her body would remain healthy and beautiful as it was now.

Every act of Gray Girl during the four-day period was ritualistic. She had often ground green corn to make the "ones-bent-over-at-the-tip," a task easy because the green corn kernels were soft. She had also worked for hours pulverizing dry corn grains between the metate and mano, a job which required greater strength, patience and skill. If the hands were not firm, the corn would not break up; if the grinding was not continued, the meal would be coarse and useless for bread; if the stones were handled awkwardly, the fingers would be bruised by squeezing. At all of these things Gray Girl was adept. Her four-day rite added two hardships she had not experienced before.

One of the features of the rite was a "sweetcake," made of cornmeal to which sprouted wheat was added for sweetening. The size of the cake depended on the amount of cornmeal available for it. The larger it was,

50

the better it would be for Gray Girl and her whole family. The girl therefore put as much time as she could into grinding. Previously she could
stop when she was tired, during these days she kept on until she was exhausted and then rested for only a short time and went at it again.

Gray Girl had many heavy silver bracelets closely set with the bluest of
turquoise. Before her adolescence rite she had removed them when she
started to grind corn. Just as food and application at the crucial time would
influence the future, so also the wearing of turquoise and silver would
bring wealth and success. Consequently she wore her jewelry instead of
setting it aside. As she bent over the low metate which was raised only a
few inches from the ground, her wrists moved rhythmically up and down
over the stone. Every time she made a stroke a bit of skin was squeezed
between the heavy bracelets as they thumped against her wristbone. She
stood the torture as long as she could, then removed the bracelets for a
short time, and conscientiously put them on again.

Persistent as she was, it was impossible for Gray Girl to grind enough
meal for the sweetcake, for it was to be six feet in diameter and a foot
thick. The women of her family, as well as those who had come to help,
ground corn for long hours. Gray Girl's competence at grinding and her
endurance at the work would make her capable and enduring in the future.
The industry of the other women would add to the effect of hers, and the
regulated and therefore beneficial use of the power Gray Girl had at this
time would reflect blessings and success on those who aided her.

Besides observing the general regulations which set the tone of her
adolescent ceremony, Gray Girl performed short rites whenever the elders
instructed her. The details of these acts had a meaning, not always obvious,
but once known always consistent with the belief that man can influence
future circumstances by repeating the reliable and acceptable acts of the
past. In other words, time for doing good or for benefiting from worthy

51

deeds is the same whether past, present or future. At the beginning of the world the Holy Ones decreed procedures and corrected mistakes due to ignorance, and after having done so, instructed man. The Navajo learned the rules in their mythology, and believe that as long as they symbolically respect the ancient acts of the gods their future is assured.

Before people were able to live on the earth, Changing Woman, the earth mother, existed. She was a goddess, beautiful, powerful, gift-giving, fertile, self-sacrificing, benign. Her existence was miraculous, for at the time she appeared there was no knowledge of procreation or birth. Two other beings, First Man and First Woman, had found her, a baby laced in a cradleboard of divine construction, on the top of a mountain. She grew supernaturally and in four days attained maturity as Gray Girl had in fourteen years. At this time First Woman had tied back a lock of Changing Woman's hair with a string made of mountain lion skin. The rest of her hair hung loose and free and for four days she did not brush it, comb it, or even push it back from her face, nor did she wash or handle water. First Woman had told Changing Woman to lie face downward on a pure white blanket of unwounded buckskin and had then massaged her body. All of these things were done to make her a comely woman.

On the first day of Gray Girl's rite one of her mother's aunts, who was respected for her goodness, but who was not especially beautiful, treated Gray Girl in the way Changing Woman had been treated, and for the same reason. Instead of an unwounded buckskin, which was too rare and expensive, Gray Girl lay on a new Pendleton blanket. After she was kneaded to make her features beautiful, she ran a short distance to the east.

For three days after the rite began Gray Girl devoted herself to fulfilling traditional requirements, but there was no public or active ritual. The fourth and last night was the time when guests were received, when in song and rite the drama of Changing Woman's nubility was celebrated,

52

when the "sweetcake" was baked. In the afternoon Silversmith dug the large hole which was to receive the cake batter. A fire had been kept burning since morning and he shoveled coals, ashes and hot sand to the side for they would be used again. The women then carried numerous buckets full of batter to the spot. They carefully lined the pit with cornhusks, poured in the batter, and covered it, in the same way as they had arranged their pit-baking for corn. When it was covered again with the hot sand they laid cedar chips evenly over the whole and then made a lively fire which was carefully tended during the entire night until dawn. A lively fire was needed because the batter was thin in consistency and deep in the pit.

Guests began arriving about dark. As they came, they were fed by a large group of women who had come to help Dezba with the cooking. About nine o'clock all those who desired a piece of the cake and who wanted to keep the night's vigil with Gray Girl had assembled in the *hogan*. The chief requirement was that they must keep awake all night. Even dozing was inexcusable, for it would lessen the effect of endurance to which end the entire rite was devoted. The fact of anyone's presence at the sing was evidence of the respect he was paying to Dezba's family. The *hogan* was so full that people almost sat on one another, and there were many who wished to get in but could not. They did not have to keep the vigil, but, wrapped in their blankets, slept on the ground outside. Those who became unbearably sleepy as the night advanced could leave the *hogan* and sleep outside, but each person in Gray Girl's presence acted as a watchman to see that his neighbors did not sleep.

When the singing began, Gray Girl, her hair loose as it had been when released the first day of her ceremony, her body loaded with necklaces, rings, bracelets, and a heavy silver belt, sat quietly at the back of the *hogan*. In front of her stood a shallow basket, three-quarters full of water, and beside it lay a piece of "soapweed," a core cut from the center of a yucca

53

root. The singers sang many groups of songs, each series devoted to the narrative of the adolescence rite of Changing Woman. Among the first of the songs were those telling of her purification by shampooing her hair in yucca suds. A group was sung as Dezba put the core of soapweed into the water and, rolling it between her palms, created foam which increased as she agitated the root and water.

The start of another group of songs was the signal for Gray Girl to put her head in the basket. They were continued as her mother helped her to shampoo and rinse her hair, her jewelry and the wide white woolen string with which she tied her queue. The basket stood for the bowl made of whiteshell in which Changing Woman had bathed. The water which had been poured into the basket from the east, south, west, north and zenith, represented black and blue rain poured from jet water bottles.

Gray Girl was grateful for the coolness and clean earthy smell of the shampoo for it helped to keep her awake. She was tired from days of labor, and the *hogan* was stuffy with its brisk fire and large audience. When the purifying rite was over there was nothing for her to do for seven hours except to listen to the monotonous beat of the songs as they took up one refrain after another in recounting one detail after another of the adolescence event in Changing Woman's life. Gray Girl had to stay awake, as did all others in the *hogan* for her sake, to pay attention to the entire recital, for on so doing the success of her future depended.

To those in the *hogan* the hours lengthened interminably. During the short pauses between the song groups cigarettes were popular, for smoking broke into the monotony. To those outside, snugly wrapped in their blankets, the hours were only moments, and it seemed that they had only dropped to sleep when they were all awakened as if to a prearranged signal. The east was gray but not light, but it was not the sun which had aroused them. Nor was it a horse or a goat tramping curiously and noisily

54

Silversmith's mother was as old as the earth itself. →

near their beds. The signal was the change in the character of the songs. For many hours the songs had continued, varied in word and somewhat in melody and tone, but withal similar in style. But with the dawn the rattles beat excitedly, the tone and rhythm quickened, a sound of great rejoicing burst from the *hogan* to greet the dawn, as the girl prepared to go to meet it.

The sleepers rose to a man and took their places with the doorway in sight as they listened attentively to the continuing song:

> She stirs, she stirs, she stirs, she stirs
> In the land of dawning she stirs, she stirs
> The white light of dawning it stirs, it stirs
> Old-age-restored-to-youth, traveling the
>   trail of beauty, stirs within her.
> Within her it stirs
> Within her it stirs
> Within her it . . .
> Within her . . .

From the first day of the ceremony Gray Girl had run a short distance from her *hogan* to the east at dawn, each day a little farther than she had run on the day preceding. Today as the visitors watched she darted from the door, a symbol of health and vitality, to engage in a real race. A crowd of half-grown boys followed as her small red moccasins skimmed the ground. Sometimes the boys let the girl win in this race, but Dezba's youngest child easily outran their best efforts as she dashed past the baking sweetcake and on for half a mile to breathe the dawn. The greeting symbolized the rejuvenation and strengthening of Gray Girl's body, even as the earth restores itself daily. The race did honor to the Sun, all-powerful lover of Changing Woman, and brought good luck to all who participated.

By the time the young people returned the women who tended the sweet-

55

← *She . . . . often washed out small pieces of clothing at the family washtub.*

cake were uncovering the pit in which it was baking. Their leader cut a piece from the center and divided it into quarters, the first of which she sent to the chief singer. Generous pieces were then distributed to all who wanted them, but the first ones went to those who had sung. Gray Girl's cake was large enough to furnish everyone with a generous portion. Each was golden brown at the edges, somewhat soggy with sweetness in the middle, but a tasty tidbit to eat at dawn or to take home and indulge in later.

As soon as the cake had been cut and passed to the visitors, they departed, leaving Gray Girl a woman, not only eligible for marriage and motherhood, but with that eligibility publicly and satisfactorily announced.

5

Conservative Son

PROBLEMS of education were very different to the Navajo twenty years ago and today. There were Government boarding-schools for Indians, a few on the Reservation, most of them far away from it. There were also some mission boarding-schools on or near their land. The Government schools provided for a number of Indian children from various tribes, not nearly enough to include all those of school age.

When it was time for school to begin, buses or trucks were sent to strategic points on the various reservations with instructions to drivers to bring a given number of children from a particular point to the school sending the conveyance. The instructions were easier to carry out in the more populous localities near the Government agencies and trading-posts and where irrigation was carried on. Most students of the old boarding-schools came from the more thickly settled regions. During the weeks when school children were being gathered, many Navajo children, osten-

57

sibly herding sheep, were really hiding in canyons and in places into which buses could not penetrate. They came home only at nightfall, and even then made themselves as inconspicuous as possible. Traders and other Whites sometimes told the drivers of homes near the road in which there were children of school age, and by various and sometimes devious means the schools were filled.

After that the Navajo children who had escaped the roundup could be reasonably content for another year, although the threat of being taken was always present. The majority, however, lived so far away from tale-telling Whites and from roads over which automobiles could travel that they were in no danger. Until quite recently many families could be found in which no individual spoke or understood a word of English.

But with the coming of motor vehicles, which have always been attractive to the Navajo, and with the consequent improvement in roads, the Indians were no longer completely isolated. The white man had many things the Indians wanted. If he did not go to them, they came to him. But he did go to them, especially to trade. Missionaries came too.

There were numerous white people in the six settlements which used to be referred to as "agencies" where the United States Government carried on its business with the Navajo. Each agency had a superintendent, offices, clerks, a school, and perhaps a hospital. Government employees worked unofficially with missionaries and there was a church or two. With headquarters at these centers there were also fieldmen, persons who were to teach the Navajo methods of stock-raising, dry-farming and irrigation. Some of these, but not many, were stationed in parts of the Navajo country far from the agencies.

Under circumstances such as these many Navajo educated their own children. When a family decided to send one or more children to white schools, they sent boys rather than girls. There was in Navajo training no

58

question or problem of education. Like Gray Girl and Alaba, a child followed the example and instruction of its elders from the time it was born. Like Dezba, her husband, and Lassos-a-warrior, the elders felt the responsibility of showing and explaining to their children every detail of their work as soon as the young were able to use it. Thus education was constant, informal and persistent.

Only late in life when a person made a definite declaration and paid a sum to bind a contract was there anything approaching formal instruction. That was when a man announced his intention of learning to "sing," that is, of mastering the exacting details which compose the ceremony chosen, so that eventually he might perform it, primarily for curing disease. And even after a man took up the practise of such a profession formally, the chanter who was his teacher, patient in explaining and in repeating forgotten points, nevertheless let his apprentice teach himself. He it was who should ask the necessary questions, he who should set the pace. If he were observant and quick-witted he could pick up a great deal simply by watching and listening attentively. A Navajo learned what he wanted to learn; facilities were his if he wanted to use them. If he did not, no one forced him or complained.

Dezba's family was representative of the transition between the old and the new. In Dezba's generation there was no doubt about the efficacy of Navajo social customs and religious practises. The old ways had been proved to be right. But the family had the modern appliances which seemed conveniences to them. Dezba was proud of her enamelled stove, but she would not have given up pit-baking. She used a food-grinder, but her daughters were all expert at grinding meal with metate and mano. Dezba herself preferred to sleep on a pile of sheepskins, but she did not criticise when her daughter used cots with thin mattresses. Although she did not undertsand it, Dezba enjoyed the music her daughter played on the phonograph she owned. The whole family wished they could have an automobile.

Gray Girl was the youngest of her daughters and Dezba had long since decided to keep her a Navajo. She would never go to school. Many material gifts of white civilization were acceptable to Dezba, but if she felt that those innovations would affect old and tried beliefs, she hesitated to adopt them.

For some reason which Dezba never understood, Tuli had begged to go to school when he was only eight. That was the first time Dezba had to consider whether her children should be conservative Navajo or whether they should be educated by white people. She had observed the results of boarding-school life on the children of her friends and relatives, and she was far from convinced that they were good. The students learned how to do a great many things the Navajo never did, but they also forgot the arts they had been brought up on. Mary, who had gone to school, was not always successful at making a fire, and her bread was often soggy. She could use a vacuum cleaner; Gray Girl did not need one.

When they coaxed Dezba to send her children to school, the white people put up many arguments. Their strongest was that "returned students" would teach their families the ways of Whites which they had learned and thus benefit their people. Dezba had seen many students who had come home, but they needed so many things the Navajo could not get to carry out their new ideas that their influence was narrowly limited. They liked to bathe every day under a shower or in a bathtub. The Navajo on the Reservation also liked to bathe, but Dezba, who was more fortunate than most of her friends, *had to haul every drop of water* she *used* at least two miles, and in dry seasons six. Similarly, she thought manicured nails, if they were not too red, were all right, but chopping splintery cedar wood, dyeing yarn, butchering sheep, and washing clothes in hard water

60

made a manicure seem futile. Dezba, like other Navajo women, kept her skin soft and her nails pliable with mutton tallow if she could not afford cold cream.

The habits which the children valued, even though not useful to the Navajo at home, did not bother Dezba as they did Mary's mother who could not tolerate her daughter's "improvements." Dezba saw no use for them, but also no harm in them. The result of "education" which Dezba dreaded most was the estrangement which grew up between children and their parents. The pupils were taken away from home. They were taught to speak English from the time they entered the school yard, and that was right. But they were punished severely for using their own language, and after they had been at school for a time they made fun of it. They came to ridicule the beliefs of their elders, and what is more, they sneered also at many of the white ways. For these reasons Dezba was afraid of losing her children by sending them to school, for she felt that to them nothing was unquestionably right.

Tuli had coaxed to go for two years, and when he was ten his mother reluctantly consented to let him go. The boys learned about building, carpentering, and machinery, and all of these could be useful to him. They also became interpreters, and there were more jobs for Navajo men who could speak English than for those who could not.

Dezba's fears for Tuli were unfounded. He had been allowed to come home for summer vacations and he always seemed glad to be home, although he had stayed at school eight winters altogether. His mother did not know that she had him with her during vacations because he was not a favorite with his teachers. Had he done his work properly, they would have kept him at school the whole year. The excuse they would have given was that "they did not want him to lose all he had learned." In reality he would have been cleaning, gardening, or laundering for them.

Tuli was only an average pupil. He learned to read and write readily. Much of his time was spent at washing dishes at which task he did not excel. He did not always wash them clean and he broke many. He could never see the need for using so many heavy dishes. When they ate at home, all used a common bowl and each person had a cup and spoon. At that he always got enough to eat, and at school he was always hungry. To him it seemed as if dishes were a substitute for food.

There were times when he had to make an endless number of beds, and he never did well at that. The job which bothered him most was gardening. The teachers kept him at it for longer hours than usual because he acted so stupid about it, and they thought he was stubborn. He had never been unwilling to hoe the family corn and beans, for that was right and useful. He had often gone on pleasant pilgrimages with his father and uncle to gather plants to be used for curing ceremonies. His father had shown him how to cut the stems with an ancient flint blade from the sacred medicine bundle and to sprinkle pollen which in itself was a prayer. His father had told him too that flowers have power, that they belong to Mother Earth and that they should never be broken without a purpose. He knew that "purpose" meant "ceremonial," that the plants were as important to a chant as were prayers, songs and sandpaintings, that their uses had been decreed when the Navajo were created, and that the decrees were irrevocable.

At the school people called the plants which his father cherished "weeds." They raised many flowers which he had never seen before and which he was sure his father did not know, only to cut them and allow them to wither in vases which were filled again and again. Enough water was used for these flowers every day to supply Tuli's family for a week, and what was it for? Tuli could never understand. He had never done well at weeding, for in addition to his reluctance to pull plants out wantonly, he really

62

. . . . *Alaba hauled wood* . . . . →

. . . . *went along when they spread salt in the troughs for the sheep.*

. . . . *her cousin who was now only nine and selling blankets of her own weaving.* →

did not know "weeds" from flowers. Instead of teaching him the difference, the woman in charge scolded him. Finally in desperation he pulled out all the little green plants.

The laundry at Indian boarding-schools was a chamber of horrors. Every child had to put in many hours there. There grew up among Indian students a special way of referring to work in the laundry, a few words uttered in a particular tone of voice with a subtle lift of the eyebrows, which was like the password of a secret society. Tuli understood the references only too well, and he never reconciled himself to the "training." He had never had a chance at the one thing he really wanted to do at the school. His fingers were skilful and he was greatly interested in machinery. All the boys wanted to be mechanics but there was room in the machine-shop for only a few. Since Tuli was not the favorite of any teacher, he was never allowed to work in the shop although he sometimes stole up to the door to watch the others at work. Then he was punished if he was caught.

Unknown to him, Tuli's ineptitude at house and laundry work, but especially in the garden, had won him his summer vacations. Summer after summer Dezba steeled herself needlessly to meet the change in him which she feared. Tuli was the smiling son she had sent away, anxious to get home, eager to herd sheep or ride the range. He had not forgotten his horsemanship, in fact he became more expert at it every year. He was always willing to hoe corn or haul wood or water, even as in the old days. He was never sulky, ill-tempered, discontented or impatient.

Soon after he came back he married a "schoolgirl," one who had the same amount of education he had. Both could understand and speak English but did so only when absolutely necessary; they preferred Navajo. Both could write, but neither liked to.

There was only one result of Tuli's boarding-school education which worried Dezba. He had married a girl of a forbidden clan. Dezba, with

63

the rest of her people, believed that marriage between two persons having the same clan-name was incestuous. Such persons called each other sister and brother, even though there was no blood relationship. Furthermore, certain clans, like Tuli's which was Black Rock and his wife's which was Red House, were closely related, and persons of the same generation called one another sister or brother. It was not quite as bad to marry one of a different clan but of the same clan-group as to marry one of the same clan, but a conservative Navajo like Dezba believed that misfortune lay in wait for those who broke the tribal rule. Dezba liked the girl, her feeling had nothing personal in it. According to her beliefs she feared the punishment which must come because the marriage was not in order. Tuli's argument that schoolboys often married even within their own clan did nothing to quiet her anxiety but rather made her apprehensive of what her tribe was coming to.

Tuli's lack of feeling about this matter was the only criticism Dezba had of his schooling. He had learned to build log and stone houses and he made his own log house comfortable and tidy by erecting cupboards and bedsteads. He had *all varieties of horsegear* which he *hung neatly outside*. Although he had not been able to work in the machine-shop, his eagerness to do so and watching the work there had given him ideas which he put into practise for the convenience of all. He devised an efficient hay-baler, made of boards and an automobile jack. Whenever anyone about the place needed construction of any kind he called on Tuli who found a way to accomplish it even with crude and scanty materials.

Even though at school Tuli had seemed to be uncoöperative, he had never been so at home. Dezba's friends and the members of her family had been able in a short time to prepare the produce of her own cornpatch for winter and had done so before the corn became thoroughly dry. About ten miles from her range lived relatives who had no sheep, but depended for their livelihood on the yield of their cornfields. For two weeks in early November Tuli spent many days with them getting the corn in. With his good wagon and team *he helped haul load after load* from fields a mile from the *hogans* in which his relatives lived. During these weeks while the men hauled corn the women husked it and *laid it out to dry in huge piles,* glistening white, dark red and pink, golden yellow, black, blue, and variegated. As a reward for his aid Tuli received several wagonloads of cornhusks, and three large sacks of corn. For some time to come *his horse which had become thin could feast.*

Although it had taught him new things, school had not changed Tuli's attitude toward his work or his own people. The innovations he adopted were not so complicated that he could not use them in his mother's environment. Besides he had not forgotten the skills he had learned before he went to school. There had been no evidence of a change in Tuli's religious beliefs. His dexterity and his interest in Navajo ceremonies recommended him to the medicine-men whom he often helped, and as time went on his intention to learn a chant became more and more fixed, although he did not act upon it formally. He would do so later.

6

Dezba's Other Child

AT THE SHEEPDIP Dezba's nephew had told the Government officer that some of the sheep belonged to "her son who was in school." This son had been named John Silversmith by the white people. As a child he had been different from the other children. Even when very young he had been the favorite of Dezba's father, a learned man now dead. John had listened carefully to every word spoken by his grandfather, especially when the words were about the history and traditions of his people. John not only remembered, but also considered carefully the instructions the old man had given. His thoughtfulness made him ask many questions, and his people were proud of his learning and his patient interest in things which to Navajo are of supreme importance.

Before he went to school John was as expert with horses as Little Policeman is today. He could ride as well as the men in a roundup, but Silversmith had never been able to put him in charge of a practical job. The sight of a barrel cactus could throw John into a fit of contemplation so deep that he forgot the stock, the purpose of his journey, even the riding itself. He would think of the story he had heard that the Barrel Cacti were people who had helped Holy Man out of a difficulty. The boy would wonder how a plant could act like a person; did it change its looks? No, for in the sandpainting it had a body like a cactus, but it had a person's head. Had times really changed so much that the behavior of plants was different in the days his grandfather spoke of, or were there times now when plants could speak to people and act like them? Could he, by constant watching, catch the cactus acting like a person?

By the time he had posed these questions to himself, and answered them, always unsatisfactorily, John would have lost the tracks he was seeking. The Navajo thought his spells of absent-mindedness amusing. No one in his family became annoyed at his blundering; they simply did not depend upon him for practical results. Although strangers laughed good-naturedly at John's lapses, his relatives, particularly Dezba and Lassos-a-warrior, looked forward to a career for him as a "seeker of the gods." His attention to spiritual things, his excellent memory, and his attention to detail gave promise that he would become a superb chanter. His questioning mind would make him thorough in correcting false ideas, and he would never get anything wrong. To him could be entrusted the highest duty demanded of a Navajo. As a chanter he would have charge of the tribal welfare. In conducting a chant without an error he would not only be able to bring success to his people, but he could even correct the mistakes they had made inadvertently by breaking traditional laws. John's prospects for the future were unlimited. After he had mastered one chant he might learn another and still another. Chanting was the career which offered the greatest rewards Navajo life had to offer, for besides power, chanters had also wealth, since one could not sing successfully without high remuneration.

The hopes for John were all based upon the precocity of a child with the assumption of training in the Navajo way. When John was nearly ten he saw children being assembled near a trading-post to be taken to a Government boarding-school. He was not satisfied with the answers to the many questions in his mind, and he was sure school would help with them. Besides, there must be many wonderful sights and experiences at the far places to which the children were taken and on the way as well. He began to coax to go to school.

Dezba was not able to refuse her children any demand upon which they had set their hearts. All the old misgivings which had tortured her when Tuli went to school were revived and multiplied. What would the white people do when John forgot where he was? Would they scold him or make fun of him so that he became afraid to explore? If they answered his queries, would the explanations lead him away from his Navajo beliefs? Would his talents be found and cultivated or would they be lost? Would he be so fired with new ambitions that he would forget the hopes of his family which he could know only by feeling? He was very young and the family had not expressed their hopes definitely. And if he found new goals, would the school give him an opportunity to reach them, or would it stop when he had only enough training to make him discontented?

The reassurance that Dezba had in the results of Tuli's education after he came home was not of great service to her when John started to school. She forgot that her previous worries had been uncalled-for. However, the fact that Tuli had survived school training satisfactorily made her consent to John's going more readily than she had when her older son left. But she could not rid herself of the doubts which obsessed her long after Silversmith had taken the boy to the school. They had delayed their decision and John started the term some weeks after it had begun.

After three months word came that a man had found Dezba's child exhausted with hunger and fatigue fifteen miles from home. The man's wife had taken John in, fed him, and would care for him until his family sent for him. His uncle went for him at once, and when Dezba saw him John seemed even frailer than usual. He had always been thin, but now his full eyes seemed abnormally large. There was an unnatural brightness in them, a puzzled seeking look which had not to do only with lack of food.

When the shock of being back in familiar, kindly hands had worn off, after the child had eaten and slept, casual questioning brought out the fact that he had run away from school. This was his second attempt. The first time he had been caught by a disciplinarian and taken back to school. Why had he not wanted to stay at the school? Why had he tried so hard to run away? The answer was simple: hunger. Never since he had left home had there been a moment when he felt satisfied. What did he have to eat? Well, at every meal there were two slices of what was called bread, something light and full of holes, and water. Every child was allowed this much, sometimes even some oatmeal without sugar, but he almost never got it. But why? The older boys were in charge of the younger ones. They also were hungry and they were strong.

One evening John had wandered off of the campus and had seen some Navajo roasting mutton at their camp. He had come just near enough to smell the broiling meat when a monitor, a boy older and larger than John, had seen him and made him come away. From that time he decided he *must* have some mutton at any cost. And still Dezba could not understand. She had always thought the white people were rich. They had big houses. They had automobiles. From them the Navajo got such silver as they had. How could those school people be so poor? John explained that they were not poor. They had plenty to eat if one were to judge by the dishes in the kitchen after every meal. Why they must have had meat! John could often smell it cooking or roasting, and he saw gravy on the dishes.

70

Laced to the babyboard little harm could come to a baby .... →

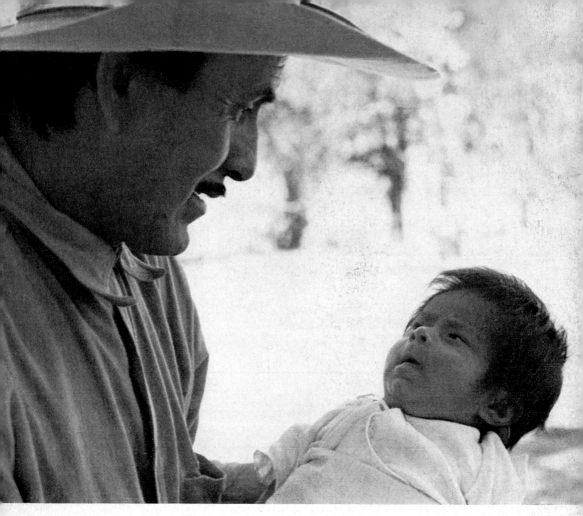

.... *Little Policeman's father must hold one of them* ....

There was no fussing if a year-old child picked up .... *a pair of scissors* .... →

When Tuli came he explained more clearly than John could, and his wife corroborated his story, that it was not because white people did not *have* food that the Indian children at school were hungry. It was because the Whites did not *give* the children enough. Now the grown children laughed at their own past sufferings for the same cause, although conditions at their school had not been quite as bad as they were at John's.

But Dezba could not laugh. She came of a people who prefaced every tale they told of the past with: "Times were hard. Deer were scarce. The people had to go far to gather a few seeds and field rats." Even though nowadays the Navajo had sheep to depend upon, there were few to whom hunger was unknown, and Dezba was not one of them. There were times when snow kept the flock so far away that no one could butcher. If the family ran out of flour at such a time, and one could not get to the trading-post, there were lean days. Dezba knew many Navajo who had no sheep to get at even in more favorable weather.

There was, however, no time during which some members of a family ate well while others looked on and had nothing. Even when rations became low, they were shared by all who would eat. If there was only one tortilla, each person had a small piece of it. There was even a story of two starving brothers who shared the last thing they had to eat, a pinyon nut. The thought kept churning in Dezba's mind: grown people eating, eating well, and little children starving before their very eyes! Her son and daughters had never lied, and the look in John's eyes was evidence, but it was a fact she would keep on knowing and would never comprehend.

Dezba took John's return and the reasons for his coming home as assurance that he would stay, and again held hopes that he might become like her brother. For two years her confidence grew and her anxiety abated, and then she discovered that the boy had run away from home to another school.

71

← . . . . *she was skilled in all her mother's arts.*

For several years she did not see him and heard of him only through vague reports of other school children. Unlike Tuli, John was a favorite of his teachers. Reading and writing fascinated him, and he spent as many hours at them as he could snatch, sometimes neglecting his other duties. He, like Tuli and all the other boys, had to put in the required number of hours at work in the kitchen, dormitory and laundry, but although he was not nearly as strong as Tuli, manual labor had little effect on him. While he was washing dishes his mind was on what he had been reading. He was naturally dexterous, and his lack of attention had few serious effects on the dishes. Although he had been taught that it was improper to destroy plants without a ceremonial purpose, he reasoned that the plants which grew in a white man's garden were different, hence the Navajo rules did not apply. As time went on he learned too the many uses of strange plants, especially the edible ones, and he became ambitious to raise some of his own. Because of his aptitude at the subjects in which they were interested, his teachers kept him over the summer vacations so that his school term lasted twelve months in the year.

In the schoolroom John's thoughtful questions were often embarrassing, for it was customary for the teachers to tell the pupils what they were expected to learn. Teachers did not encourage questions, for too often they themselves did not know the answers. At times they found John's moods, which changed frequently, disturbing and inconvenient. Nevertheless his avid learning, his excellent memory, and the eagerness of his winning smile made the annoyance of his unusual temperament short-lived.

He did not come home until the middle of the fifth summer after he had left. Although he was talkative and admired the rugs being woven and said it was good to have the old food to eat, there was about him an air of detachment. He had a kind of aloof elegance which was out of place. When Dezba read his face, she was convinced that his affection for her had not changed. John looked at Lassos-a-warrior with admiration and respect, but he seemed to sit on the very edge of a sheepskin, hardly touching it. He drank gingerly from a cup, or even used one of his own which he carried with him and lent to no one. He had brought a blanketroll with him. He refused the sheepskin Dezba offered him to sleep on and the next day complained frequently that he had not slept because the floor was so hard. He was sure he would get a cold. The men thought his remarks funny and teased him, for they believed that one became strong through sleeplessness, as they demonstrated at vigils such as that which they had kept with Gray Girl on the last night of her puberty rite.

As a baby John had had firm delicate hands, and during his childhood he had finished everything he made fastidiously. Dezba was pleased to note that his fingers had grown sure and strong. She had noticed that many school children, in contrast to Gray Girl, did things swiftly and carelessly. When they tried to make a fire, instead of making it neatly pointed with just the right draft, they let it straggle untidily over the fireplace. Often the little pile of wood collapsed before it was properly ignited. A hasty child set the coffeepot uncertainly in the fire so that it upset before it boiled. Another tied a knot which immediately pulled loose. The hands of these children were weak and uncontrolled, they did not follow the eye and mind. Dezba in watching her son had no fault to find with his manual skill. Just by watching him she knew he had continued in his old way and age and strength had aided his progress.

John was amused and surprised when Dezba showed him the flock she had painstakingly guarded with his brand. He was accustomed to considering himself a poor Indian schoolboy who had none of the things he desired, such as pencils, paper, drawing pens and books. He was also used to thinking that because he had no cash at all there was no way to get them. He had never thought of himself as a sheep-owner. He was proud of the

73

family's large herd of cattle, but when he joined the men to cut out a yearling for butchering, he complained unendingly of the hard two-hour ride with them.

John had visited Dezba only a few days the first time he came home, but he made it a point to come again before the summer was over. After that for many years he came more frequently when he had short vacations. It became clear that he would not, soon at least, come back to the Reservation to stay. He had become so accustomed to white ways of living that he could not tolerate Navajo discomforts. The white people he knew always had work for him to do, and often it was work he liked. Besides, there seemed no limit to his need for learning from books and paper, and he always had plans to continue his studies further.

One day as John sat watching Dezba weave, she learned, to her surprise, that he too could weave. At school, he told her, he had passed through the hall where Navajo girls were being taught weaving by a white teacher. He had noticed and remarked about a process which was different from the Navajo way and, he thought, inefficient. The teacher had appealed to him to show the class how to do it, and from then on he had taken up weaving in order to teach others. He explained to his mother that there were many other crafts which could be learned at school. He liked modeling, wood-carving and painting, and had worked some at each of them. He set no value on the things he had made. They were kept at school. They were not his.

Dezba knew he had never woven at home, although he had sat beside her for many hours simply watching. He had done the same when his father was making silver, and one time during a visit he asked his father to let him try to fashion a buckle. Silversmith was astonished to see him handle the tools properly, and finally turn out a buckle with a complicated design as good as he, an experienced smith, could have made. Similarly,

74

John's sister reported that her brother had casually picked up his brother-in-law's awl and had made a perfect pair of moccasins.

John's talents and his expertness pleased the members of his family as they became acquainted with his preoccupations. As time went on and his career progressed, his habits became further and further removed from theirs, yet his attitude toward them as persons seemed ever more loving. At the same time he grew more contemplative and speculative. During his years at school religion had fascinated him as much as it had puzzled him. By the time he had left home he had come to understand many of the beliefs and teachings of his people. At school he was required to attend church, and he became interested in comparing the religion of the Whites with his own. For some years he had been a nominal Protestant, then out of curiosity he became a Catholic. As his education progressed he was led to explore all kinds of new and exciting trails. In trying to cast Navajo belief into the form of philosophical definition, he became greatly dissatisfied with his information. The old chanters had taught him what to do in carrying out a chant and when to do it, but they had never told him why they believed and acted as they did. He was sure more knowledge held the answer to the many questions for which philosophy groped, and he returned to his mother's home for an entire summer to "study with" Lassos-a-warrior, to continue instruction from where he had left off ten years before. To Dezba and his uncle he had become a "seeker of the gods."

7

Play

I T WAS IMPOSSIBLE to say when Alaba and Little Policeman
played and when they worked. They were responsible for herding and
watering the sheep, but while they did these things they played. Alaba
even played that she was herding and watering sheep. When she joined
Tom, the herder, to help him give salt to the flock, or when she patted
dough into a tortilla for Gray Girl, she did not consider she was working.
Nor when she first shaped enough tortillas and baked them for the family
meal without any help did she think she was playing. Little Policeman
herded on horseback because he was old enough to be trusted with the
large flock. Alaba went on foot and envied her cousin his responsibility.

When Tuli rounded up cattle or there was a branding, he expected his
son to ride as hard as the men and valued his help. To Alaba who was a
tomboy, Little Policeman's horsemanship was a source of envy, a pleasure
which was denied her. It was taken for granted that he should ride like

mad, wave his hat and shriek, swing his rope, throw and tie a calf. It did not matter to Little Policeman that at the end of the day he was dead tired from the work he had done. The days he found trying were those when he had no horse with which to work with his father. He missed the ride in the sunny sage-scented air. He would play no part in the dusty tussle with a calf struggling for its freedom. He had been left at home tending sheep like a woman. Only at times when there was excitement elsewhere, even though hard labor went with it, did Little Policeman consider a placid job like herding work.

Branding concerned the women of the family as well as the men. After the cattle had been rounded up and driven into the corral a mile from Dezba's home, the women drove up in the wagon, and the branding, like other kinds of labor, turned into a bee. Only the family were present, but there was the movement, the color, and the laughter which made all gatherings fun. As the men in the center of the corral twirled their lassos and shouted the women anticipated their needs and ran up with a branding-iron, a bucket of water, or a knife at the exact moment it was needed. The women also composed an audience to encourage the men. The miss of the loop or a clever saving of a throw brought exclamations of ridicule or congratulation. A calf or a steer, thrown but not tied, which got away, was a joke. Branding was a short, exciting interruption of daily tasks. Like sheep-dipping it was necessary hard work. With it much pleasure was intermingled although it was only a family affair.

Every member of Dezba's family loved a crowd, but none was at a loss if he had to be alone. Even though her family was large, there were many hours when Dezba was by herself. When alone she was likely to weave, for weaving was an occupation she could not take visiting with her, even to her daughters' houses. She never felt lonesome, for there were too many things in which she was interested. She enjoyed the glossy smooth-

78

Gray Girl . . . . always had a rug on her loom . . . . →

. . . . had to haul every drop of water . . . . used . . . .

← *. . . . the food-grinder was (a modern convenience).*

ness of her old batten, notched and polished by constant ramming between warps, and the balance of her favorite weaving comb with exactly the shape and weight to fit her hand comfortably. She was proud of the strong hard warp and the fluffy even yarn which she pushed to and fro between the warps. As the rug became larger, she became more and more interested in the pattern. Sometimes she found it better to change the design she had in her mind when she started, and then there was the quiet suspense of seeing how it would come out.

Her range was a source of constant satisfaction. *When at sunset* she sat outside awaiting the return of her family, *she could hear the song of a rider coming up over the hill and the sheep bleating toward the corral.* The range furnished fodder for them, she could depend on the earth. It was one thing she was sure of. The sheep gave her lambs and wool which she could sell. With the wool she wove into rugs she could obtain ready cash. The logs of her *hogan* were cut from her own land, and she did not have to go far for wood to keep her warm. From early morning when she breathed the sharp, night-washed air until she stood behind her house at sunset she realized the pleasure of possession of wooded hills and fruitful earth.

Dezba did not think of her daily tasks as work or play. She had always done them and she expected to continue doing them. She did not even consider whether or not she liked to do them. If there was too much to do, Silversmith's mother, Gray Girl, or someone else helped her. Although she was never idle, neither was she over-worked. Although she sometimes set a date for the finishing of a rug or a skirt, she was only slightly disappointed if she did not finish it by that time.

Dezba's people did not consider it proper to leave women, and especially young girls, alone. Yet the conditions of their life were such that Gray Girl was sometimes the only one who could herd. The men were haying, Tom

← . . . . *all varieties of horsegear . . . . hung neatly outside (the house).*

the herdboy had been hired by a white man, Little Policeman was attending the day-school nearby, Alaba was too small to tend the herd alone. Gray Girl, like Dezba, did not feel lonesome when she was left alone. It might even be that sometime a gay-shirted rider would visit her as she roamed alone, or when she sent Alaba over the hill. Visiting a herdgirl was one of the few occasions a young man had for private courting.

There were many times when a Navajo man expected to be alone. *Silversmith worked alone for many an hour.* Tuli drove his wagon for water and alone filled the water barrels. Lassos-a-warrior, the chanter, rode long miles to the top of the mountain to gather the petals of dainty blue flowers which grew only there. Alone he rode long distances when he was called upon to perform one of his healing chants. When he had learned the chants, as a "seeker of the gods," he had secured power by keeping solitary vigil for a whole night at a time, and often he had to be alone when he prayed. Night is the time when danger, because it is indefinite, lurks more thickly than in the daytime. It was not "good" to do things at night, but it often happened that the sun arrived home before a lone rider, and then the traveler spurred his horse as he sang a high-pitched song to keep undefined evils out of his way.

Although Dezba's family did not think to separate work and play in their daily life, and carried on their occupations with good humor and pleasure, there were times when no work was involved. Recreation meant a large gathering of Navajo and there were many occasions for it. If a "party" for the Navajo was given or organized by white men, it was called a "chickenpull." The name came from the Spanish game in which there was a contest of riders who tried to capture a rooster buried to its neck in the earth. Three things were necessary to the success of a Navajo chickenpull. *There must be* many people in attendance, *a large amount of food to eat,* and a rodeo. In addition, there were often other features such as

80

exhibitions of handcrafts, stock, farm products, and dances, and usually there was a Squaw Dance at night.

The greatest of these gatherings was the famous Indian Tribal Ceremonial at Gallup which occurred annually the third week in August. It was arranged by the businessmen of Gallup and had features of entertainment enjoyed by Whites as well as those of Indian origin. Indian tribes as far away as Oklahoma and Wyoming sent dance troupes. There were also affairs on the Reservation which, although sponsored by white men, were run by the Navajo. One of these was the Navajo Tribal Fair which was held only thirty miles from Dezba's home.

One day Tom came home announcing that the date for the Tribal Fair had been fixed for the middle of September. No one in Dezba's family had attended the Gallup Ceremonial except her brother who had led a prizewinning dance. The three household heads decided that all the family should go to the Fair, except of course the herdboy, for someone would have to take care of the sheep. Several days before it was time to leave, household interests became subordinated to preparations for the Fair which would last three days. The wagon with all provisions for a five-day absence would start the day before the Fair began and arrive home the day after it closed.

Silversmith started off on his horse to find his racing stallion, grazing on the range no one knew where, for it had not been seen for weeks. Dezba's married daughters started stitching new skirts for the women and shirts for the men. Gray Girl restrung her whiteshell and turquoise beads to wear and arranged a set of matching silver earrings, bracelet and necklace on a velvet pad for the exhibit. Dezba, who had a rug half-finished, worked industriously to finish it for her entry. At intervals between the sewing and weaving, the women prepared food. They made a batch of the "ones-bent-over-at-the-tip" and baked many small loaves of raised bread. *They killed a sheep* and cut up the meat so it could be carried in sacks. There had been no word that the Government which sponsored the Fair was going to provide a feast, and it was better to take along enough food to make sure all would be fed. Members of the family would of course visit and eat at the camps of their friends, and similarly, friends would come to Dezba's camp.

The day before the Fair, just before the wagon started off, Silversmith rode up triumphantly driving his stallion before him. Tuli was pleased, for he would ride it for his father. Tuli, Silversmith, and Lassos-a-warrior rode to the Fair driving their racer and a band of other wild horses from the neighborhood.

Gray Girl drove the wagon in which rode the women and Little Police-man. Today there were no faded clothes such as those they had worn to the sheepdip, but every woman wore her gayest, fullest skirt, and her new-est velvet blouse. Each also wore her best Pendleton blanket which covered the brilliance of her dress but added its own brightness. Alaba had her blanket too, but hers lay neatly folded on the seat. She moved about too much to tolerate the binding of her shoulders and besides, the day was warm. Temperature made no difference to the women. It was simply a custom as binding as a law: *without a blanket one* was not completely dressed, *one was not going anywhere.*

Alaba was much excited to be going on this trip, and not nearly as en-vious as usual of Little Policeman, for he too was riding in the wagon. His hat, a two-gallon imitation of his father's four-gallon Stetson, hung rak-ishly on the back of his head. It indicated that a man was fully dressed, as the Pendleton blanket did for the women. A silk cerise handkerchief, also exactly like his father's, was knotted around his neck. In his arms he hugged a puppy. He did not dodge back and forth in the wagon as did Alaba, for he had brought his lasso. He put it on the wagon floor and kept

82

his foot on it every minute so he could be sure of its whereabouts. As they drove along he made remarks which kept the women in a constant state of laughter. He did not miss a bird or a prairiedog that flitted or scurried from under the horses' feet. He wondered if the prairiedog "ladies" had made new skirts for the Fair and if the jack rabbits would enter the races.

After sunset the party made a camp on the top of the mountain where there were tall yellow pines. There was luscious grass for the horses, and Dezba showed the children a spring. *Coffee was made* and sheep ribs were broiled, and there was a sackful of hard-crusted bread. As the fire flickered down, each one slept comfortably wound up in her blanket.

When *the men* arrived at the Fair the next day just after noon they *found their wagon in the midst of a large encampment.* Around each vehicle sheepskins and blankets were spread and every family had a fire. For three days hundreds of Navajo would make themselves at home here.

The first day was devoted to preparations. Exhibits came in gradually as one wagon after another joined the camp circle. Every man, woman, and child visited the stock show time and time again. There were entries of wiry horses and bulls with a treacherous look in their eyes. And above all there were sheep and goats. There were old-fashioned Navajo sheep with soft ripply fleece. There were huge Rambouillets with heavily folded layers of wool, displayed as examples of what Navajo sheep could develop into, given the proper opportunity. There were Angora goats and milch goats. There were even a few highly bred pigs in which the visitors showed little interest.

A hoganlike building housed a model day school with desks, books, and teaching equipment of the most modern kinds. But it was not a place where there were merely things. There were Navajo children learning as they actually did at the day schools which had been introduced to the Reservation a few years before.

83

The exhibit hall was large and showed off rugs, silver, and farm products to good advantage. Many hours were spent by the Navajo looking, criticizing, picking up new ideas.

A rodeo was scheduled for every afternoon at two o'clock, and one o'clock saw the roomy bleachers which had been built into a hillside crowded with spectators. The first day it seemed that the events were being rehearsed. Many entries were late coming in, groups were assembling to work together, starts were repeated again and again. The organization was similar to that of the great pageants belonging to the Navajo sings. People lived far distant. They could not get together for preliminary rehearsals. There was no exact moment when all could be expected to be present. However, given several days for the crowd to assemble, coöperation took form like magic. Small groups agreed to perform together and started to practise, and soon they had developed an act. If the man who promised to come did not arrive, someone else did, and he was substituted. Or if many came who were unexpected, they became as thoroughly welded into the whole as if elaborate arrangements had been made beforehand.

Thus it happened that the invisible machinery of coöperation had, by the second afternoon, assembled a performance that was colorful, fast and exciting. Long before two o'clock Dezba's family had found excellent seats in the center of the bleachers. They were surrounded by hundreds of Navajo, who were always able to move up so there was room for more, even as they were at home in a crowded *hogan*. When seats were no longer easily available, the late-comers sat on the sloping hillside into which the tiers of seats had been built.

The arena was a half-mile track with corrals and chutes for the animals in the center. The Fair Grounds were chosen so that at the east there was a backdrop of red sandstone rocks of the "haystack" type. The scene was set. The audience was ready. Little Policeman, his feet again resting on his

84

lasso, and Alaba, both silent, were among the most excited of the spectators. The greatest event to them would be Tuli's race on the black stallion,
but every incident, even though frequently repeated, interested them anew.
There was the grand spectacle of the entrance parade when hundreds of
horsemen rode in single file, curbing their mounts to a dignified walk.
Little Policeman noted especially the long rhythmic line of lassos, tied
to the many saddles. The riders were *followed by* hundreds of *covered
wagons,* filled with showily dressed Navajo.

After the entrance which was slow and dignified, events followed with
breath-taking speed. Races, quarter-mile, half-mile, mile and two-mile,
were won and lost. Between them came bronco-riding, the broncs demon-
strating every twist known to the most expert cowboy. Navajo rode wild
bulls, forward and backward. There were bull-dogging and contests in
milking wild cows, the most amusing of all the events. In all of these contests there was a large number of entries, and every man who wished to
ride, throw, or milk was allowed to try. To the Navajo onlookers, whether
adult or child, there was no such thing as too much repetition. If nineteen
boys had ridden broncos, to them the twentieth was as exciting as the first,
if not more so. If a man had gone to the effort of bringing what he thought
was a "mean" animal for a try, the fact that nineteen other fellows had
done the same did not furnish grounds for elimination.

If to the Navajo audience there was zest in monotony and repetition,
there was also gusto in surprise, surprise not so much at the newness of an
act, but astonishment at the skill with which it was performed. Little
Policeman thought that for him his father's race would be the climax of
the day. Events were so numerous and succeeded one another so fast that
he forgot to make his usual sage comments. He was completely overcome
with amazement, however, when a famous roper from a far-distant tribe
put on a solo performance. *Tuli had many excellent rope tricks, and Little*

Policeman imitated them, but the variety and difficulty of the stranger's tricks were so amazing that the boy rose from his seat to find out how they were done. It seemed only a moment until they were all over, and Little Policeman sank back in his seat breathless. To his regret and that of his father they were not repeated, nor was there another roper. Perhaps the same man would perform tomorrow.

Alaba had not missed a detail the entire afternoon, nor was she less thrilled than Little Policeman. If anything her excitement was greater. She was learning to ride, of course, but when she had become as expert as her grandmother she would be expected to ride serenely and sedately, for Navajo women were above all things dignified. There would be no yelling and hat-throwing, no exuberance of spirits, but always quiet control, even as today, when Alaba had uttered hardly a word.

The women's events consequently were to her the high spot of the day. Seven women competed in a mile race. Straight-backed and sober-faced they sat, their horses at the line. They had left off their blankets, and their ruffled skirts were snapped to their ankles like a bicyclist's trousers. At the signal they were off. They leaned forward as the horses increased in speed. With moccasins but without spurs, with hands and quirts but without hats, the determined quiet women egged on the horses and the race was one of the great successes of the day.

Alaba became hopeful of an eventful future once more when two large groups of women took their places on opposite sides of a long rope for a tug-of-war. She bet aloud on the north side because on it there were three very fat women. After a long determined struggle, amidst laughter and dust, the south side won. It did not matter who won, but Alaba secretly resolved that she would join in sports of this sort when she grew up.

She dreamed of a future more eventful than that of her grandmother and aunts as the men rode broncos and tied wild calves. Then suddenly it

86

. . . . he helped haul load after load . . . . →

. . . . *laid it out to dry in huge piles* . . . .

. . . . *his horse which had become thin could feast.*

Photograph by L. J. R.

When at sunset . . . .

was announced that a young Navajo girl would ride one of the wild bulls. This, to Dezba as well as to Alaba, was unheard-of. Nevertheless after some suspense, a girl who could in no way be distinguished from a boy broke through a gate riding a protesting bull. To Alaba this girl had reached the peak in accomplishment and as she vowed to emulate her, she heard her grandmother say to the woman sitting beside her, "That girl has always acted exactly like a boy. She has never worn a dress in her life. It may be all right for her, because she goes to school and acts just like a white girl. But I would not like to have one of my girls act like that. Such sports are too rough for women."

"I wouldn't let my girls do such things either. And I keep them away from the dancing too. Of course many of the girls dance, but I do not want to get money that way, and when a decent young man asks me for one of them I shall be able to tell him, 'She doesn't dance.' "

Dezba's friend referred to the so-called "Squaw Dance" which was a part of a three-day "War Dance" given frequently on the Reservation. At the Squaw Dance a young girl invited a young man to dance with her and the dance continued until the man paid her a coin. Many mothers taught their daughters to solicit dances when they were still very young, and those same mothers pocketed the takings. Dezba and her friend did not consider the custom respectable, although it was very general. It happened occasionally that the most desirable young man in a community asked his parents to choose for him a woman who did not dance. Dezba and her friend hoped to get husbands who would make such a stipulation for their girls. In spite of the comments of the women, Alaba still thought she would like to dance.

The rodeo ended with a chickenpull for which there were many contestants, among them Tuli who had won third prize in the horserace. Instead of a live rooster, the Navajo used a sack of sand buried in the track so that only the top protruded. Where there had been order and regularity,

87

there was now confusion and scrimmage. Before the audience could realize what was happening, Tuli rode out of the close huddle of horsemen waving the sack, and he, the defeated competitors and the audience broke into shouts which closed the rodeo.

The Fair Committee had prevailed upon a group of medicine-men to perform the nine-day ceremony called the Mountain Chant. They had held it near the Fair Grounds, timing it so that the last night would coincide with the last night of the Fair, and because they were doing this they requested that the usual Squaw Dance be omitted, since it was not "right" that both should be carried on simultaneously. The entertainment of the last night consequently consisted of a display of talent which was Navajo in every respect.

The Mountain Chant was one of the most elaborate of the Navajo curing chants. It was not performed very often because of the great expense which attended it, expenditure necessary not only to pay those who helped carry on the chant, but also to feed the vast number of visitors. During the first eight days the chanters, for the benefit of a man who had been ill, had "sung over him." That is, they had carried out the rigorous ritual of the chant, every act succeeding every other in an order which had been specified in ancient times and which was handed down in myth. They had sung many groups of songs, all in prescribed order. They had purified themselves, the patient, and all who wished to participate, by sweating four times near a huge fire and by taking an emetic. The patient had been further purified by a bath and shampoo in yucca suds. Since the Navajo believed that the gods could bring healing if they were properly importuned, the chanters had made "prayersticks" of various kinds of wood upon which they painted designs peculiar to the deities being invited. When these objects had been properly made, prayed over, and deposited in places the gods could not miss, the gods could not fail to come.

88

They came in the form of sandpaintings, one made during each of the four last days of the chant, and each representing some occasion upon which the gods had helped a sacred hero who in mythological times had had the same troubles the present patient now had. When the patient sat on the painting he absorbed the power of the god or of the sacred hero. The ancient hero had been restored, the patient would be restored. There were many details of the performance, each as important as every other for the patient's welfare, and every one was carried out conscientiously by the chanters. Most of the rites were done in the presence of only a few people. Anyone who so desired could enter the ceremonial *hogan* for the time during which the sand from the sandpainting was applied to the patient's body, symbolically making him a god. On the last night an elaborate summary of all the songs, acts, and rites included in the nine-day chant, as well as in the myth which explained it, took place. To this all-night summary all were invited, and this was the occasion which closed the Navajo Fair.

Within a huge circle made by laying green branches in place there was room for many small fires. Near these fires family groups made themselves as comfortable as possible on sheepskins and blankets. In the center of the circle a great pile of wood sent flames twenty or thirty feet into the sky. A wide track between center fire and audience was kept open to serve as the stage and in this open space the dancers and tricksters performed. There were many chants in the Navajo repertoire, each differing from the others, not so much in general pattern as in details and symbolical significance. Each chant had a symbol of costume and dance by which it was represented during the night. The entire night's performance was named for the setting in which it was held "Dark-circle-of-branches."

When the fresh fire sent flames high into the sky and heat far out at the sides which formed the stage, nine or ten men, their nude bodies painted

89

thickly in white paint or clay, advanced stealthily toward the fire, emiting queer arresting sounds. They carried sticks tipped with eagle down, and as they stole up to the fire and retreated quickly, they at first tried in vain to ignite the feathers. For some minutes they failed, making much business of their attempts and the failure of their efforts. At last one and then another succeeded in lighting the eagle down which of course burned off instantly. Then with more pretense and clowning the actors miraculously replaced the down and repeated the performance.

The feathertip burning act was followed by arrow-swallowing. Six men took part in this. Their bodies were naked and painted and they carried long feathered arrows. As they danced about in the firelight making great pretensions for their powers, they swallowed the arrows including the stone point up to half their length, *i.e.,* about twelve inches. When the actors pulled the arrows out, neither arrows nor actors' throats showed adverse effects.

Another act was dainty as well as clever. Eight men, once more with the body paintings characteristic of the chant they represented, danced out, holding large flexible arclike properties strung gracefully with eagle plumes. After dancing in a line, they paired off, and the first of a pair set his arc on the head and shoulders of his partner. The second, balancing the arc on his own head, placed the arc with which he danced on the head of his partner. So each dancer performed until all heads were fitted with the swaying feathery headdresses. All danced again keeping the arcs in place balanced by head and shoulders, no longer touching them with the hands.

To Alaba and Little Policeman the most wonderful dance of them all was the Fire Dance by which name the entire night's performance was usually designated by Whites. Both children hoped they could keep awake long enough to see it. Sometimes it was early on the program, sometimes it closed the night's performance. They had had an exciting day. The fresh

90

air, the smoke and the flickering of the fire made them very sleepy, but they were lucky, for the Fire Dance followed the Dance-of-the-standing-arcs.

The many Fire Dancers were heralded by a loud noise. Painted or daubed with white clay they ran into the arena bearing long bundles of shredded cedar bark. Before their entry the fire had been renewed with huge branches of dry cedar. These dancers, like those of the first dance of the evening, made many fruitless attempts to light the cedar bark from the central fire. Finally their leader succeeded, then each one lighted his torch, either at the fire or from the bundle of a fellow-dancer. When all were burning the dancers ran around the fire with them. Their purpose was to bathe the bodies of the dancers in flame, but if a runner got too far behind the one in front, he ran the flame of his torch over his own back and down his legs. They continued until the torches were burned out when they dropped the short remains on the ground and ran out of the light. After the performers had left the stage, those of the audience who wished to do so, among them Dezba, rushed to pick up a few of the cedarbark ashes. These they took home to serve as a cure for injuries due to burning.

Soon after the Fire Dance was over, the children were sound asleep, and the audience became gradually smaller as the Whites left for their homes or the Navajo for their blankets near their wagon camps. There were, however, curious Whites who wanted to see everything, and numerous Navajo who, like Dezba and Lassos-a-warrior, believed they would derive benefit from seeing the chant through until dawn, as was the custom on the last night of every chant. These remained interestedly awake until the final play.

The acts continued with varied details the night through, and since a large number of troupes had responded to the invitation to perform, the intermission between dances was not long. Many of the dances carried out exactly the same steps, the variation being in costume and the symbols carried in the hands. In one the headdresses were feathered and spruce boughs were carried in the hands. In another the dancers carried tall elaborately-constructed frames from which dangled ribbon streamers.

Instead of dancing in figures, some of the actors performed tricks. Two eagle feathers danced in a basket surrounded at a distance of four feet or more by a chorus of men who sang to the rhythm of rattles. The sun was made to rise and set without apparent help. One group of men bathed their hands, just as they would if washing them, in burning pinyon gum. The final act of the night's show, performed just before dawn, was the trick of the yucca fruit. A group of actors entered the circle, amongst them two who behaved like clowns. After giving their cries and circling the fire several times, all but the clowns formed a semi-circle at the west. The clowns performed a great deal of funny business, then all closed the circle for a moment. When it opened a yucca root had been planted in the sand. They repeated the act, and the second time the circle opened a yucca plant was growing there. The third time the plant had its high stalk of creamy bell-like flowers. And when the circle of men closed and drew apart for the fourth time, the plant stood large and complete with small green fruit hanging in a cluster like bananas from the stalk.

As the cold white light of morning preceded the yellow sun, the dark circle was emptied. The ashes of the small fires lay blue along the edges of the corral and around them adults as well as children slept soundly. Most of the families retired to their wagons where they snatched a few hours of sleep until the hot rays of the sun, the flies, and the dust and noise of packing aroused them. Then sleepily the women lighted the fires, warmed some coffee and reached for cold tortillas. Within three hours the wagons, automobiles, and horses had disappeared, leaving as the only evidence of a three-day vacation the litter of watermelon rinds and a few bones too well polished for even the dogs' interest.

8

Singing

DEZBA was brought up to believe in the relationship between man and nature sustained by ceremonial order, that order attained by song. She had never known any other religion and there was no confusion in her faith. In her youth she had been strong, healthy and full of energy. When she was about thirty-five she began to lose her ambition. She had frequent severe headaches. She had little appetite and became very thin. Although she slept a great deal more than a Navajo woman should, she always felt tired. For some months the symptoms continued, her condition remaining much the same with no change for the worse, none for the better. At last Silversmith and Lassos-a-warrior, after themselves considering all the possible causes of Dezba's illness without arriving at a satisfactory conclusion, called in "one-who-can-see," a person who has the gift of prophecy by means of star-gazing.

This man, with Silversmith and Lassos-a-warrior, repaired to a lonely spot on a hill one starry night. The seer stretched out his arms straight in front of him with his palms covered with pollen. To the accompaniment of song he gazed steadily at a large star until his hands began to tremble. As he concentrated on the star, the trembling spread to his whole body and caused him to make motions with his hands as if they were trying to draw a rough pattern. Soon the motions and quivering of the body ceased. The man then brought not only his gaze, but his whole being back from far places. He passed his hands slowly over his eyes, and once more became himself.

He then told the men who were with him that Dezba ought to have the Beauty Chant sung over her, for the involuntary motions of his hands had outlined one of the sandpaintings belonging to that chant. He did not say why that particular chant should have appeared. He recommended that it be sung at once, and he added, that if after a few months, she was not better, it should be followed by the War Dance.

Lassos-a-warrior at once engaged a Beauty Chanter, and within a few days, the five-day form of the chant was sung with Dezba as patient. She was purified by drinking a decoction, by violent sweating, by bathing and shampooing her hair in yucca suds, and by drying her body with yellow cornmeal. She had lotions applied to her and sprinkled over her. By means of prayersticks, prepared and offered with prayer, the gods were invited. In the form of figures painted in sand they came. With song and rite the parts of their bodies were applied to the same parts of her body, making her one with them. During the last night when she did not sleep at all, the songs of the preceding nights and days were reviewed and repetition in perfect order added its charm to her cure. Conscientiously Dezba carried out all the requirements of the chant and the taboos against working for four days after it was over. She seemed to feel somewhat better for a few days after the chant was over, but she still did not have enough ambition to start to weave. The fact that she had not woven a blanket for over

94

. . . . she could hear the song of a rider coming up over the hill . . . . →

. . . . and the sheep bleating toward the corral.

Photograph by L. J. R.

There must be . . . . a large amount of food to eat . . . .

a year was one of the most alarming of her symptoms. Not long after the sing was over, she felt as ill as she had before.

For three months, as the diviner had recommended, she trusted to the power she believed in, hoping that the chant would still cure, but she only dragged along and became weaker until the family prepared to have a War Dance with her as patient.

The War Dance differed from the chants in certain ways. It was sung over a person to counteract harm which had come from strangers. Two groups of people, living a considerable distance apart, participated. Each group represented one side of the warring parties, for it was believed that harm which came from enmity could be cured by symbolical fighting. On two mornings a large quantity of gifts was given away, one distribution taking place at the headquarters of each of the opposing parties. The exchange of gifts denoted peace-making. More time during the three days' duration of the War Dance was given to public performance than in the chants. The public acts of the War Dance were entertaining and dramatic, although they always retained some religious significance. The so-called "Squaw Dance" which was almost wholly social, was danced in the afternoons and continued throughout the nights.

Dezba, as the patient for whom the War Dance was given, did not share in many of its secular parts. She spent every moment carrying out the ritualistic instructions just as she did when a chant was sung over her. At the time when a scalpstick was being contested for by the "warriors" for her benefit, she was secluded. The rites which were performed over her simultaneously with the war play going on before the large audience of visitors, were similar in most ways to those of the chants. *Dezba,* sitting *in a shade,* was blackened with charcoal from head to foot so that the enemy could not recognize her. In every respect according to traditional description, she was made identical with the great god of war, Enemy Slayer, and

← *Silversmith worked alone for many an hour.*

by being so treated attained his powers. The only ones allowed to see the rites accomplishing the identification were warriors or those who had symbolically become warriors from having previously been patients for whom the War Dance had been performed.

The large chorus which accompanied the public performers sang many songs in falsetto. The singers had had no special training in singing song series, but had voluntarily joined the chorus because they liked to sing. Those who sang over Dezba as she was dressed to represent the war god were medicine-men who sang in low tones songs in which word, note and order were of great importance. Their singing was like that of the chants and its purpose to make her into another, a supernatural being. It was believed that the secular music in falsetto helped in restoration. It was even thought that such high-pitched music could bring a person out of a coma or faint. The combination of "War Dance song," that is, falsetto, with "chant song," that is, low-toned song in series, would increase the chances for Dezba's cure.

After the War ceremony was over and Dezba had rested from its vigil, she continued to feel weak. Rheumatism added itself to her other complaints.

Before she had become ill, Dezba's trader-friend had given her credit on a large rug he had ordered her to weave. She had started to spin the yarn for it, but had made no progress. She had not been able to "see" a pattern. Without a design she had no incentive, nor could she judge how much yarn of each kind she would need. From time to time the trader had asked her how she was getting on with the rug and she had put him off by joking or changing the subject.

When he came to see her sometime after the War Dance was over he was shocked to find her emaciated and unable to move her hands except with great pain. For some years he had wondered how anyone with teeth as bad as Dezba's could be healthy. The trader was a man who never hesitated or did things by halves, and as he was leaving he said, "I want you to come with me. I am going to take you to Gallup and get those teeth pulled. Then I am sure you will get well."

Dezba demurred, but the trader never took "no" for an answer. Before she could realize what was happening, she found herself, wrapped in her newest blanket, riding beside her friend, bound for the dentist's. She could meet her own gods with equanimity, but she trembled, as did the seer when "seeing," as she considered the drastic cure in store for her. When the trader arrived at Gallup with her, he called the dentist who was his friend, and in no time, all of Dezba's teeth had been extracted. The trader stayed with her during the ordeal to interpret for her, then took her to his home to recover. The next day he drove her home.

As her gums began to heal, Dezba found herself becoming hungry. She even enjoyed the tortillas dipped in broth or coffee, and it was not long before she was able to eat meat. After several weeks her brother suggested that she have a "little sing," one lasting only one night. A chanter came, sprinkled pollen, and sang from nine one night until dawn of the next day.

Dezba continued to improve in health. Two months after she had been at Gallup she went to the trading-post where she saw the trader. Earnestly now and with eagerness, she told him that she had come to buy dyes, for the yarn for his rug was spun. As he got out the dye he remarked upon her cure, and was silently congratulating himself as having brought it about when she said, "Sometimes those-who-see make mistakes. The one who trembled for me said I ought to have the Beauty Chant. I had it but I did not get any better. Then I had the War Dance and that did not do any good. I just kept getting worse. Then finally a chanter sang the Blessing Chant, only a one-night sing, over me, and now I am well. Often the little sings cure after the big ones have failed."

. . . .

97

Dezba did not depend upon sings for restoration only after evil had taken possession of her, but she believed in them also as a preventative. After she had recovered her health and taken up her weaving even more vigorously than before her illness, the trader discussed a new undertaking with her and her brother. For years this friend of theirs had felt that the sandpaintings which were a part of the ceremonies were too unusual to remain a form of art unknown to the world in general. Made as they were with dry natural-colored sands, it was not possible to see them in their entirety for longer than an hour at most. Even that privilege was given to only a few who were not Navajo, when by good fortune, they happened to be present during the brief moments the public was allowed in the ceremonial *hogan* while the painting was being used. The trader knew of the firm belief that the sandpaintings should not be made permanent, that their power should be learned and retained only in the minds of the chanters. In talking over the matter with Lassos-a-warrior, he gave his reasons for wanting a permanent record of the sandpaintings. He wanted that record in two forms. He would show the chanter how to paint with water colors and he wanted Dezba to weave a rug exactly like the painting.

Lassos-a-warrior was so confident of his own power to prevent harm by his knowledge of chant lore that he did not hesitate long in trying out water colors for depicting his sandpainting designs. It was customary to pay large sums for any knowledge of supernatural control and the trader offered a good price. Besides, after the chanter had gained control of brush and paint, as he did very quickly, he found the work quite as fascinating as the painting of prayersticks which was also a part of his profession. Brushes for painting them were made of shredded yucca fiber and paints were of ground colors mixed with water. The surface, being a cylinder of wood, was more difficult to paint on than paper, even though the lines did not have to be as exacting as those for the sandpaintings.

98

Once the sacred designs had been carried out on paper, anyone having the skill could copy them. Dezba had the skill. After long discussions on the subject with her brother and husband, they came to the conclusion that it would be safe for her to weave the designs of a particular chant, if first she had that chant sung over her. The decision was quite consistent with the belief that formal application of the chant requirements to a person rendered him immune to any harm which the powers invoked by the chant might otherwise bring. For instance, if the Thunders imparted their power to the one-sung-over in the Wind or Shooting Chant, never would thunder or lightning harm that person.

Accordingly Dezba consented to weave a sandpainting rug for the trader. His first watercolor paintings were from the Shooting Chant, and Dezba was the one-sung-over during a nine-day performance of that chant. She found it difficult to weave the first sandpainting design she undertook, not only because the arrangement of the details was more involved than anything she had ever done before, but also because she had to overcome her fear at fashioning the sacred figures. It took her nearly two years to finish the first rug of the kind, even though she worked at it industriously and her relatives helped her to spin. Nevertheless the weaving proved profitable, for in no other way could she earn the large sum of money she was paid. And, like her brother, she became so engrossed in the work itself that she wanted to try another. She felt sure she could improve greatly on the first. The flight of time, her interest in the difficult art, and the compensation she received gradually made her forget her apprehensions about the wrath of the Holy Ones and she came to trust in the power of the chant to protect her.

As the years sped by the trader collected a large number of sandpainting designs. Some of his favorites were from the Wind Chant, and before Dezba started on one of those, she first fortified herself by becoming the

99

one-sung-over during a nine-day version of the Wind Chant. By this time Dezba's friends were accustomed to her weaving the Holy Ones and only rarely did she have to meet criticism against it.

During a long and busy life, interpreted in terms of her belief, experience confirmed Dezba's faith in the teachings of her people. She herself, as well as many of her friends and relatives, had tested the value of ceremonial and found it successful. It was no wonder then that she brought up her children to understand and trust in the same way. Now the children were grown and had given Dezba grandchildren old enough for training.

A bright crisp day at the end of November found the family once more on its creaking way in the reliable wagon. This time they were bound, not for a working bee or a chickenpull, but for the chant which had been ordained as the greatest of them all, the Night Chant. The most important character of this chant was Talking God, who was also called *yeibichai,* or "grandfather of the gods." For this reason the chant itself was often called *yeibichai.* It was one which all Navajo, whether they lived near or far, made great efforts to attend. But to Dezba and her family there was on this occasion an additional incentive besides the pleasure and benefit attendance involved.

Alaba was to have her first real understanding of what her people mean by deity, for she was to be initiated for the first time. During her babyhood and early childhood she had been treated exactly as an adult. When she was only three weeks old, her mother had taken her to a sing. Pollen had been placed in her mouth and on her head as her mother whispered a prayer for her. When the time came for everyone to hold a piece of sacred flint while a long prayer was offered, the baby's hand was made to touch one also. At another sing, when she was only three years old, everyone was told to walk around the fire stepping over pokers, starting with the right foot and alternating with the left. Alaba did her best to put the right foot

100

forward although she did not know one from the other, and everybody laughed at her. Since that time she had obeyed commands to perform many ritualistic acts, but today differed from them all. Then she had tried to do as she was told. From today on she would be responsible for her own acts, for she was "to see the gods."

Every Navajo sing had some theme which was stressed, and around which the action moved. In the Dark-circle-of-branches the performances of visitors, that is, typical dances from other chants and even from neighboring tribes, were stressed. In the War Dance the effects of enmity and the treatment of enemies constituted the theme. One form of the Shooting Chant centered about the Sun and his home. The Wind Chant featured the Wind People. The *yeibichai,* or Night Chant was the dance of the masked gods. Talking God was the leader of the many gods who appeared, and as usual, the dances of the last night presented a summary of the helpfulness of them all.

Talking God, among the many gods, had been the chief bogeyman of Alaba's childhood. He was able to do anything and would punish naughty children. He was the more wonderful because, in spite of his name, he did not talk. He merely made a sound *"wuhu, wuhu, wuhu, wuhu"* which was terrifying and compelling. He had had his name since mythological times when by means of words he had communicated with adventurous and wonderful heroes.

Alaba was one of a group of five females and four males, among them Little Policeman. Because he was older than Alaba, the rite was his second and he had no fear of it. Until a person had been initiated, the identity of the gods was a secret which not even a young child would divulge under threat of deific punishment. Children took pride also in having a secret the younger ones could not share, in being part of a grownup mystery. When elders were neglectful or poor, their children were sometimes not initiated until they were grown and responsible for their own safety so that there were adults in the group as well as children. Alaba and Little Policeman who belonged to a Chanter's family, were started on the course when young, for their elders believed it to be safer so.

On the fifth night of the ceremony the leaders had made their preparations, which to Alaba waiting, had seemed to require an endless amount of time, and the groups of children were called into the ceremonial *hogan*. They had first been carefully instructed to keep their heads bowed and their eyes hidden in their blankets. The boys marched around the fire to the back of the *hogan* where they sat in a group and began to undress as men must do for divine communication. The girls sat in a bevy opposite and merely let their blankets fall from their shoulders.

During all this time the gods stood in a line facing the novices and hooting in a frightening way. Talking God, accompanied by another called Female God, led them. After the boys had stripped, Female God advanced and applied sacred pollen to various portions of their bodies. Talking God followed and struck them with a wide yucca leaf. The two gods then approached the girls who sat with downcast eyes. Female God applied pollen to them also, and Talking God held specially prepared ears of corn, tied with spruce twigs, to their feet, knees, outstretched palms, shoulders, chest, back and head, as he gave his cry *"wuhu, wuhu, wuhu, wuhu."* Once more the Chanter told the initiates to keep their faces and eyes hidden.

Then the gods laid the masks on the ground and bade the children look up. They raised their eyes to behold, not the frightening visages they expected, but the kindly familiar faces of their fathers and uncles. The tall grotesque figures they had feared were not the gods themselves, but only impersonations. The revelation helped somewhat to dispel the fear which Alaba had carried like a cold stone in her heart for days. The initiates saw that Female God, the mate of Talking God, was impersonated by a man.

They killed a sheep . . . .

After surprising the children by showing the disguise, Female God placed "his" mask directly over their faces in turn, making sure the eyes of each initiate looked out clearly from the holes of the mask which represented eyes. If he had not been careful about this, the child whose eyes were hidden might have become blind.

The next act was to sprinkle pollen over the masks in the most exacting fashion. The larger children and adults did this according to instructions, the little ones like Alaba had their hands guided. In this rite it would not do only to try to follow directions, the directions must be carried out accurately. If the novices accomplished each motion with a prayer, they might attain the dearest wish of their hearts. They were to sprinkle pollen around the eyes of the mask. The child who slipped some into the eyeholes might become blind. They were to sprinkle pollen downward over the nose of the mask to produce rainfall. The child who sprinkled it upward might cause a drouth. The pollen was to be sprinkled upward over the cheeks of the mask. The child who accidentally dropped the powder downward might hinder growth, not only of the crops, but even of himself. No child wanted to be a dwarf.

When the rite had been completed to the satisfaction of chanter and parents, Alaba was gathered lovingly into her grandmother's shawl. Sleep thawed out the fear under whose sway the little girl had lived for many days. From now on, sworn to secrecy regarding uninitiated children, she could talk to Little Policeman about Talking God and his companions. Since her cousin had been twice "whipped," he was twice as safe as Alaba in viewing sacred things. To be completely guarded from harm both children must go through the rite with four different sets of masks, that is masks belonging to four different Night Chanters. After that they might look upon the most sacred sandpaintings or altar pieces with safety.

All of the exacting rites had been performed for eight days to make the

103

. . . . without a blanket one was not going anywhere . . . .

Night Chant successful. The dancers had practised for hours during the preceding days and nights. As the sun set on the ninth night, the visitors took up their places in two long rows extending east from the ceremonial *hogan*. Large fires of cedar and pinyon marked the lines which bound the wide stage where the gods were to gather, fires close enough together to warm every one in the audience during the sharp cold night. The audience visited while they waited. They had food and cooking utensils with them and during the long intermissions they boiled coffee and broiled meat.

At intervals long lines of tall men, painted, costumed and bemasked, danced up toward the *hogan* door in front of which the one-being-sung-over sat or stood. Some of the visitations were marked by long prayers delivered by the Chanter, and during these times the audience was silent. The patient faithfully sprinkled the impersonators with cornmeal, as the actors acknowledged the offering with their peculiar godlike calls. One of them represented the water god. He was called Water Sprinkler and he acted like a clown. He tumbled foolishly, sometimes vulgarly, near the audience, carrying out in ribald mockery the sacred acts, and mimicking the holy words of his serious companions. Alaba drew back perceptibly whenever he came near her for she found it hard to remember that the being beneath the mask was only her "father's brother."

As usual on the last night which is called *"the* night" of a sing, the audience kept vigil. The dances continued, the fires died down, were replenished, flared up. The audience visited and ate, the children slept. During intermissions speeches were made. An old man begged the audience to contribute to a fund to get his son out of jail. A young man spoke in behalf of a candidate who was up for election to the tribal council. At last the night was gone. When white streaks, so pale as to be only a promise of dawn, showed in the east, the concluding song, the Bluebird song, dedicated to the herald of the dawn, rang out:

He has a voice
He has a voice
He has a voice
He has a voice.

Just at dawn *Sialia* calls
The bluebird has a voice
Having a voice, his voice is melodious
His voice being beautiful, gladly it flows
Sialia calls, *Sialia* calls.

. . . .

Confidence in the ways of her people and in her own concordance with those ways was the secret of Dezba's tranquillity. During the sixty years of her life she had met many of life's vicissitudes. By following through the complicated order of ceremonies which had been ordained, by laying on of hands, repetition of prayers, purification and vigils, she had so reinforced her innate self-reliance that nothing could disturb her serenity. With the sanctions of the great or masked gods, secured through the Night Chant; with the protection of thunder, lightning, snakes and arrows, acquired in the Shooting Chant; with the aid of beings of the air brought by the Wind Chant; and freed from dangers which strangers could bring her by the War Dance, Dezba had the assurance of enjoying the harmony which is above all the spirits, subterranean, terrestrial and ethereal. Not only she, but all except one of her children, and now her grandchildren, were also included in that accord. The token of glistening olivella shell, which with a small but perfect turquoise bead was tied to her hairstring indicated her close relationship to the spirits. With these weapons intrepidly she walked the trail of happiness.

9

Authority

LASSOS-A-WARRIOR was born while his parents were on their way from their old home in northeastern Arizona to Fort Sumner in eastern New Mexico whither the government scout, Kit Carson, was herding the Navajo in 1863. For many years there had been killings and reprisals affecting Whites and Navajo. For many years soldiers had tried to subdue the Navajo. Until Christopher Carson, who had learned warring from the Indians themselves, was put in command, all attempts had proved futile.

Carson knew that Canyon de Chelley was the natural stronghold of the Navajo. *The precipitous walls of the canyon were a better protection than forts.* The floor of the canyon was a garden, for there the Indians raised the bulk of their food, corn, beans, squash and peaches. There were many living springs, and water was close to the surface of the river channel even when it seemed dry. The caves of the canyon were natural storehouses for

107

large emergency supplies. The Navajo at this time had enough sheep for their own use and some horses. Carson knew that they could be overcome if their food supply could be destroyed. But what was more important, he knew how to get his own soldiers into the Navajo country in such a condition that they could rout the Navajo. Other parties of soldiers had been defeated by their own fears of thirst and starvation even after they had traversed miles of the unfriendly desert and were nearly in sight of their objective.

Carson invaded Canyon de Chelley with his soldiers. They captured horses, killed the sheep, and burned the food. Then they rounded up such of the Navajo as had not hidden, or as could be found by desultory searching and drove them like animals over the long desert route they themselves had come. The women and very small children were allowed to ride in the wagons. Boys of six or eight were too proud to ride in the overcrowded vehicles, and marched, staggered rather, beside them for dreary miles.

Under these circumstances the mother of Lassos-a-warrior made out as best she could. Not long after the birth of the child an accident occurred which was to deprive him of virility. After many weary days they reached Fort Sumner, then called Bosque Rodondo, where the Navajo were kept for four years. They were inured to hardships like hunger and thirst which the American soldiers could not endure, but the loss of their freedom and the idleness demanded by their captivity took a heavy toll.

The earliest childhood of Lassos-a-warrior was spent in an atmosphere of spiritlessness and futility which left an indelible impression on his memory later reinforced by oft-repeated tales of the elders. The Navajo at Fort Sumner were sad and gloomy. The food was different from that to which they were accustomed and many, especially children, died before they got used to it. Here it was that they first learned to drink coffee, eat wheat bread and beef. They pined for their homes, but more particularly for their freedom. With liberty they could, then as now, have found and founded new homes. A few worked for wages for the Government, most of them sat "with folded arms." There was no incentive to work, no work to be done. The second year things became somewhat better for they made small gardens and began to assimilate, if not to savor, the strange food. Food was rationed every three days, and necessities like clothing, dishes and tobacco, every two months.

During the four years they stayed more and more Navajo were driven in until the census recorded nearly eight thousand. A few escaped, usually to be destroyed by hostile Indian tribes who lay between their prison and their home three hundred miles to the west. Finally after four years Navajo leaders agreed to cease raiding. The U. S. Government gave up the expensive conquest and allowed them to go home. The journey back was beset with difficulties of all sorts and took its toll, but the Navajo were not driven. They had the hope most precious to a people who even today insists upon individuality, their freedom, the right to do as they pleased as long as they did not please to attack white people. The Government had given each Indian some sheep and a few cattle. They could now look forward to wandering once more with their small herds on their own land. They could see green cornfields against the dark red canyon walls. *They could call upon their gods at the White House,* a place they believed the gods had chosen in ancient days for divulging to the Navajo the precious healing secrets of the greatest of their chants. It was a journey of hope instead of desperation.

There was no doubt about the memory of one event of the journey in the mind of Lassos-a-warrior even though he was only four when it happened. His family had become more and more hopeful as they expected in a day's travel to reach land with every stone of which they were familiar.

A sudden sally made by three Utes on the wagon robbed the family of a strong handsome fifteen-year-old girl. The father was of course unarmed. He did what he could with the help of his older sons to save his wife and the children. On the eve of arrival in his own country he had to swallow the chagrin and shame of seeing his oldest daughter taken captive.

A few years later he learned that his daughter was living as the wife of a Ute near the boundary between the Navajo and the Ute territories. He had by this time reestablished his home and become prosperous. With several of his clansmen Lassos-a-warrior's father set out to get his daughter back. The girl had never forgotten her people and had run away twice, but had been recaptured. Her father's party sneaked as close as they could get to the Ute camp without detection. They waited until the Ute men had all left the camp, then by signals had the girl wander away from the house. When she was far out of sight of the old women of her husband's camp, she mounted a fast horse her father had brought for her and before the Utes discovered her escape, the Navajo party was on the way home.

A long time after, in order to avoid attack and further bloodshed, the girl's father negotiated with a friendly Ute to settle the feud. Her Ute husband was paid eight horses for the loss of his captive wife and the Navajo had no more fear of attack from that quarter.

As he grew Lassos-a-warrior never refused the work assigned to boys, in fact he did everything expected of him. But when he matured, although he became tall, his body was slender and delicate. Ordinarily his companions would have made fun of such an effeminate boy, but they all knew he had been injured. To call attention to a defect might well be to put themselves in the way of sustaining the same affliction and they were taking no chances on that. Then too from earliest childhood the child had had an air of gentle dignity which set him apart and made him immune to all jibes.

110

Coffee was made . . . . →

. . . . *the men* . . . . *found their wagon in the midst of a large encampment.*

. . . . followed by . . . . covered wagons . . . .

His name had nothing to do with either his appearance or his behavior. When his sister had been recovered from the Utes, his father had given a big War Dance to free her from alien harm. It was among the first of the sings given after the Navajo returned from imprisonment, for the first years had been devoted to hard work and resources were too limited to pay the medicine-men. For a long period children had not been given sacred names, names which constituted a charm, for by mentioning a name, a person could get himself out of great danger. At the War Dance sung over his sister, Lassos-a-warrior, with a group of other children, received his name. It was believed that daily use of such a name would wear out its power, and it was not until Lassos-a-warrior had become acquainted with white people that his "war name" was used regularly.

The Navajo called persons of his type *nadlay,* which means "one-who-changes." Individuals who "change" are generally men who prefer women's activities to those of men. Accordingly, they either give up the work men customarily perform, and do women's work, or they occupy themselves with women's work while not giving up entirely those things in which men are interested.

Lassos-a-warrior had enriched his life by adding weaving to his accomplishments. His weaving and the fact that he did not marry were the chief reasons he was called *nadlay.* But instead of giving up singing, which was usually a man's profession, he dedicated his life to it from early youth. He had acquired a large flock of sheep. Besides talent for management, Lassos-a-warrior had become famous for the unusual and intricate patterns he wove and which sold for high prices.

Before he was thirty he realized that there was no satisfaction in wealth for itself, for he took no joy in the acquisition of material things. He had already begun to learn to sing, but he finally made up his mind to give up everything for religion. Accordingly, he paid a generous fee to a

III

← *Tuli had many excellent rope tricks . . . .*

Mountain Chanter who was his instructor. Then he divided his property among his female relatives, his mother, his sisters, and his sisters' children. From this time on, although riches came his way easily, he retained little for himself. When he was paid for singing, he gave most of the fees away. He kept only a few horses. A wiry nag with endless endurance did him service as he rode to and fro from chant to chant.

The fact that he had no family obligations left him free to concentrate on his chosen calling. He did not learn it piecemeal as most chanters do, but devoted all his time to it. To do this he apprenticed himself to a man who lived far distant, not for a winter, but for five consecutive years of intensive application. When he was convinced he had learned what that singer had to teach, Dezba's brother moved further and stayed two years longer with one who practised a different branch of the chosen chant.

The attainment of wealth through skill and singing was enough to merit Navajo respect and admiration, but Lassos-a-warrior, like Dezba, had more than that. He had a confident composure which nothing could disturb since he feared neither man, nature, nor even the supernatural. He was as much at home with Talking God as he was with Alaba. To him one was as wonderful as the other. The strength of his belief was apparent in the folds of his face. *There was a mellow simplicity with a strong touch of humor and* a great deal of *forbearance.* His vivacious eye and his gentle manner gave to all the comfortable feeling of complete understanding. To him there was no sin, only ignorance or weakness. Had the Holy Ones not ordained the order which would allow every tiny cog to slip into place even though at times dislocated? Had he and others not learned to restore that order? The impression of secure stability which he gave had no relationship to asceticism, for no one participated more actively than he in mundane affairs. His philosophy of life was mystical, but without human affairs, it would have had no reason for existence.

112

When people were afflicted, puzzled, or uncertain they came to him, and even when he came to the same impasse they had reached, they felt some assurance because the conclusion had been arrived at by authority.

The parents of a wealthy girl belonging to the Mud clan were greatly troubled by events following her death, and came to Lassos-a-warrior for advice. Her mother's uncle and a friend of the family known as Black Moustache, had carried her body to the grave and with it they had deposited a sack containing silver jewelry and dollars. They did this because the silver was one of the girl's intimate possessions and the family wanted to show their respect and love for their child by not using it. About a year afterwards Black Moustache became alarmingly ill. A seer took omens to determine what chant would cure him. As he gazed, the trembling which shook his body became so violent that it nearly threw him. His mouth went dry and his song died out to a moan. It was a long time before he could gain sufficient control of himself to murmur, "The stars show that Black Moustache stole the valuables which were buried with the Mud clan girl."

The seer had to recover from the shock of his discovery as well as from his concentration, for Black Moustache was a good friend of his. When accused, Black Moustache denied the theft, and no chant could be prescribed.

The relatives of the deceased girl, already grieved by the death of their child, were so upset by the betrayal of their friend, Black Moustache, that they could not accept the decree of fate without further discussion and they brought their trouble to Lassos-a-warrior. They believed that the illness of their friend proved his guilt, and besides, the seer would not have accused his good friend without more than natural knowledge. After the family's delegates had told every detail of the story, not once but half a dozen times in different words, Lassos-a-warrior was forced to conclude,

"My friends, there is nothing you can do. If he does not confess, there is absolutely nothing."

This convinced the party and they returned home with heavy hearts. The mere charge that he had taken what had belonged to the dead set Black Moustache apart as a wizard. His illness became steadily more alarming until he consented to the soothsaying once more, this time by a man he did not know. This one came out of his trance with the verdict that the sick man had robbed a grave, and only then in his extremity did the accused own up. The chant against witchcraft cured his illness. The return of the valuables wiped out his crime. As Lassos-a-warrior had said, there was no hope for the case except in the sufferer himself.

Because Dezba's brother had given up his own property, he was regarded as being fair and reasonable in matters regarding that of others. The relatives of Lone Cedar, an old friend of Lassos-a-warrior, came to him after Lone Cedar's death, not so much to get advice about their difficulties as to have Lassos-a-warrior confirm their judgment and announce it with conviction.

The death of Lone Cedar was a great shock to Dezba's family, for it had happened suddenly. Not until Lone Cedar's sons came to Lassos-a-warrior did they know the cause. The eldest son told the story: "My father had been as well as usual and there had been no sign that he was ill. He came in and sat down in a spiritless fashion. You know he was customarily lively and talkative. He did not eat when we had supper. After the meal, when everybody was sitting around, he suddenly said, 'There is no more hope now. I am going to die.'

"Everybody was too surprised to say anything and before we could catch our breath, he went on speaking very quietly and we realized he was making his will. He gave directions about all his property. There was nothing we could say. Before morning he was dead.

114

"Now we have come to you, our friend, to ask you to help us about this will. Some parts of it agree with Navajo custom, but some are more according to white man's laws. We want to carry them all out as well as we can, but we have relatives who will complain and we came to ask you to talk to them so they will not make a fuss."

Lassos-a-warrior said he would do what he could, and the young man explained the circumstances. Lone Cedar had been a wealthy chanter. Much as he had cared about his sheep and his dollars, he had considered his knowledge his most precious possession. Like all medicine-men, he had wanted to teach some young men, and because he had many sons and grandsons, he would have preferred them as understudies. Although Lone Cedar had done all he could to encourage them, only one, his "grandson," that is, his sister's daughter's son, had shown any interest in learning from the chanter. The boy's name was Slim Navajo. Not only had he been willing to concentrate properly, but he had rare intelligence and had become Lone Cedar's favorite. To Slim Navajo, Lone Cedar had willed the bulk of his property.

The son who had come to Lassos-a-warrior explained that Lone Cedar's sister's sons who were a generation older than Slim Navajo might object to having the younger man get so much while they were to receive only a little. Furthermore, against Navajo custom, Lone Cedar had bequeathed ten sheep to his wife, and ten sheep and a cow apiece to his own children. His sisters and their families might object seriously to these bequests which would take the property out of Lone Cedar's clan and apportion it as white people do. Since some of Lone Cedar's children had been educated and did things according to white ways, the father had made his will thus so they would not go to the white court about the estate.

Although theoretically there were certain relatives, a man's mother, sisters, brothers and their children, that is, the members of his clan, who rightfully inherited from him, actually those persons who attended a family gathering shortly after the burial were the ones who secured the property. Often remote relatives, or those with whom the deceased while living, had had little to do, turned up at these meetings in large numbers. All had a right to take something away since they showed their respect for the deceased by coming. Lone Cedar's sons requested Lassos-a-warrior, who was only a remote relative, and who would not expect anything, to speak to those who assembled regarding his father's property. As they rode to Lone Cedar's home, the son repeated that his mother and his brothers and sisters were very anxious to carry out his father's wishes and they wished to prevent, if possible, argument and litigation. To them the oral will was as binding as if it had been written before a lawyer and signed by a dozen witnesses.

When the two arrived at Lone Cedar's home the expected large crowd of kinfolk was there. Lassos-a-warrior greeted them in his quiet friendly way, and as soon as they were ready to start the meeting, he began to speak in an earnest low tone. All listened attentively to every word. He dwelt for some time on the good deeds and high character of the deceased. He cited times when he himself had benefited greatly by the helpfulness and wisdom of Lone Cedar. He went on to outline the old-fashioned Navajo course of action at such a time.

"But," he continued, "although ordinarily you could all expect to inherit according to your relationship and to your presence here at this gathering, today things are somewhat different. Our friend made a will, to it the members of his family were witnesses. To you, his wife and his children, he left some stock. I hope this will cause no dissatisfaction on the part of his sisters and brothers and their children, for he did it to satisfy the law of the white man. On the other hand, you, his wife and children, could fight for a larger amount in the court at Fort Defiance, but I hope that

116

you will not dishonor the memory of your husband and father by trying to change his last wishes or by dissension of any kind. To you, his nieces and nephews, he left a goodly sum, and it is to be hoped that you will be satisfied with it, rather than try to get something away from the young man, your nephew, to whom he willed it.

"He had a good reason for doing so. Had you wished, you yourselves, any of your own children, or his own sons could have been his followers. Nothing would have gratified him more than to have had more than just this one to instruct. But you did not. You preferred to go about freely. You did not want to be tied down with responsibility for singing. Now that your nephew has done this, and you will all agree that he applied himself faithfully, is it not reasonable to let him also reap the reward of his attention, since this is the way his grandfather wished it to be?

"For the sake of respect to our friend, I beg of you, be bound by his word, do not let the private affairs of our brother be taken to the white court where they will surely be settled in a way strange to us, and certainly not according to his wishes. A number of you are here who were not mentioned by him. Try not to be too disappointed that you are not to carry much away with you. Enjoy the good feast which has been provided for you. Eat all you can and then feel assured you have respected in the highest sense the will of him who did so much for you when he was among us."

In words which left no room for argument Lassos-a-warrior had touched upon all the points having to do with the case. He had done so with such force, authority and finality that everything which was being done seemed right. The listeners had the feeling too that the old man himself had no stake in the decision, and they accepted the will exactly as it stood.

Doubt and confusion were not the only difficulties Lassos-a-warrior was

117

called upon to dissipate. His friends sometimes drew upon his talent for graceful speaking to break good news. John Whitehouse had gone to school, and while there had married a girl from a foreign tribe. They had lived on the Navajo Reservation where they had brought up a large family. Both of them were Christians, John having become an active missionary. However, their livelihood depended, as did that of most Navajo, on land and sheep, for preaching did not pay well. With help from many directions they had even sent some of their children to college. Then came a period of misfortune. Two of the children had died, and Mrs. Whitehouse had to raise the four orphaned grandchildren who survived. Suddenly in the middle of the summer when John was only fifty, he was stricken with pneumonia and died.

Mrs. Whitehouse being a foreigner, even though she had lived among the Navajo for thirty years, had no one to turn to. Ordinarily her husband's sisters and brothers would have inherited, not only such property as he possessed, but also his responsibilities, and his children would have been cared for. But John Whitehouse had neither relatives nor property. He had had rights to use ten acres of irrigated land. But since it was not customary for spouse or children to inherit from husband or father, there was grave question as to whether John's family would succeed to these rights.

The widow feared she might have to return to her own tribe where she no longer had a place. Only a few years before she had gone back to visit her people to satisfy a longing for home. Her stay had impressed her with the poverty of her own people who were desert people without flocks. She had not remembered how little they had, how hard they had struggled to keep body and soul together. Many of her friends had died. Her nearest relatives had become pitifully old. She had found no common tie even with those her own age. The thought of returning to her own people

118

. . . . and Little Policeman imitated them . . . . →

Photograph by L. J. R.

Dezba (sat) in a shade (especially built) . . . .

made Mrs. Whitehouse desperate. She could see no way by means of which, try as she would, she could manage to feed the four small grandchildren and herself.

The neighbors of the Whitehouses were wealthy, and they lived in a valley where there was cordial coöperation even among the Navajo of conflicting beliefs. A number of the influential men put their heads together, and when their meeting was over, they had a plan which they asked Lassos-a-warrior to communicate to Mrs. Whitehouse and her family. There was another family council, but the outsiders at this one had come to give, not to take.

The speech of Dezba's brother was short and simple. It began with a rehearsal of the qualities of the deceased, then came to the point, "Your husband was one of our children. For some years his beliefs were different from ours. That makes no difference, a child of ours is always a child of ours. Many years ago you were a stranger who came here to live among us. You learned to speak our language. You bore children for our people. You and they have had a long run of misfortune. That sometimes happens. The only thing left to do then is to help out. Perhaps soon your children will be able to help you. These people want me to tell you that until then they will do what they can to help. They wish to let you use the ten acres of irrigated land which belonged to your husband now deceased. This man here will bring his horses to work it and these others will give you labor. This woman offers to take care of your sheep along with hers until you can manage them yourself. Maybe in this way you can get along."

119

10

Return to Earth

IMPERCEPTIBLY the beautiful green summer merged into fall, the autumn lengthened into November with the sharp clarity which lifts the sky to twice its usual height and etches every line of the cliffs, every leaf of the evergreens, every blade of vegetation in perfect focus. The season was satisfactory to all. *The sheep were fat, the wool was thick and sleek,* the corn and beans plentiful. It was a year when the crop of pinyon nuts was large. Many members of numerous families had spent the month of November at the pinyon camps where one and all, large and small picked, tiny nut by tiny nut, the carloads which were shipped from Gallup. Favorable weather had lasted a deceivingly long time. The nut-pickers returned home and set off with new provisions to pick more and larger sacks full of the fragrant oily tidbits. Christmas day saw nearly all returned for the many celebrations given by the various trading-posts and missions.

Just before New Year there was a Mountain Chant which Lassos-a-warrior attended. Before it was over a wind came up bringing with it such a heavy snowfall that many who had intended to go were prevented because the roads were impassable even to their sturdy pintos. The two hundred guests who had already assembled went on with the feasting and ceremony, disappointed that more could not come for the Fire Dance, but otherwise unperturbed. They had to stay several days longer than they had intended, but a quantity of meat and flour sufficient to feed the anticipated crowd had been provided and feasting continued even after the ceremony was over. Every day the men, and with them Lassos-a-warrior, put forth their best efforts to open the roads, first to riders and later, when the snowplow came through from the highway, to wagons and cars.

When Lassos-a-warrior arrived home his bones ached and he had a bad cough, fever, and headache. He said he was a little tired from the hard work and would just rest a little. His fever lessened after two days and in two days more he was better, but surprisingly weak. By this time a War Dance had been started eight miles from his *hogan* and, although Dezba suggested that he stay home, he jokingly wobbled onto his horse and started off. The biting air, the soft deceit of the snow, the azure sky stimulated him, and as he rode, he thought how foolish people are. Why! These are the things which restore, not the inactivity of rest which can only weaken! As he rode and contemplated the landscape, every blemish of which had been metamorphosed into radiance—an old stump was a fluff of down, every spike of homely Russian thistle a baby star, the red mesas had turned to mahogany coated with ermine, their pockets become blueberry frost—he started as usual to sing. But the notes stuck in his throat throwing him into such a paroxysm of coughing that he had to dismount. He recovered himself only with difficulty and had to lead his horse a long way because he had not the strength to mount. When he arrived where

122

the crowd stood about the huge fires, each man turning himself as if on a spit, Lassos-a-warrior almost fell from his horse and at once went into the house of the host where he sank upon a bed of sheepskins.

He said, and the others agreed with him, that he was only exhausted from the work and the ride in the snow, but as the sing proceeded even into its third day, he was not able to get up, daggers had taken possession of his chest and back, fever of his brain. He was too weak to express scorn for his own debility when gentle hands lifted him into a wagon spread with soft comfortables. At home he consented to have a doctor and Silver-smith went for one, but the doctor and Lassos-a-warrior's best friend, the trader, were miles away. They had been completely snowed in before they could get back from the Christmas vacation.

The thin wiry frame of Lassos-a-warrior had survived an incredible amount of abuse since the days when it had come into existence on the way to Fort Sumner. It had been pushed and harried and disciplined. Until now it had been unswerving in service and endurance, until now it had come through successfully in health and dependability. At last too much had been exacted. It could no longer sustain the indomitable spirit which bore it. When he was too weak to talk and breathing became diffi-cult, Lassos-a-warrior signaled to his sister and nieces to take him outdoors and they had the men move him to a small unused *hogan* not far from his large one. Here he settled down on the sheepskins as his relatives first stood silently about, then gradually glided away, leaving only Dezba who knew of nothing to do for him but to hold his hand and wipe his forehead. Death did not come, Life went.

With its going, the being which had been quietly but no less effectively adored by its kin became to them an object of abject unreasoning fear, of dread which reduced every one to impotency. It was the Dead. Few, if any, Navajo were afraid of death; fewer, if any, could overcome the

123

phobia which possessed them in the presence of the dead. Ordinarily the missionary or the trader was called upon to bury, and usually one or the other obliged. Today the trader was gone. There was only a clerk in the store who had never before come to the aid of a Navajo and it would be useless to send there for help. The road to the Mission was so deep with snow that no one would travel it to bury an Indian. There were several clans whose members need have no fear of the dead, nor do the dead contaminate them, but none of these lived within calling distance now that the roads were closed. There was only one thing to do—Silversmith himself would have to attend to the burial of his brother-in-law.

He called upon Tuli and Dezba's two sons-in-law. Loco had not been there, but had ridden over as soon as he heard of the family's sorrow. Silversmith appointed him to choose a place for the interment. He ran two miles to a canyon to the east, choosing his trail as far as possible where the snow had blown away. There he selected a crevice well protected from water and difficult of access, even to animals. Near it were many loose stones which could be used to close the opening of the grave and to hide it from prowling eyes.

While he was gone the other three men stripped off their clothes as they would have done to imbibe power in a chant, but now they rubbed their bodies with ashes to ward off undefinable evils at the thought of which they cringed. They even untied their hair strings and let down their hair. Their every move was calculated to prevent as far as possible the contamination which results from contact with the dead. They bathed the fragile corpse with yucca suds and dressed it in the purple velvet shirt and white trousers their owner had worn at celebrations. They put on his necklaces and bracelets which he happened to have got out of pawn to wear to the chants he had recently attended. They laid the body on its possessor's best and gaudiest blanket and beside it they strung his belt of heavy old conchas. They laid out also two other blankets, a silver bridle which Lassos-a-warrior had recently received in payment for a sing, and his medicine bundle. They saddled his favorite horse.

They had not quite finished these preparations when Loco returned. When all was ready, the goods were packed upon the saddle and the entrance to the death *hogan* which was at the east was sealed. Tuli and his brother-in-law cut a hole through the north side of the house and out of it the corpse was carried. Then they burned the *hogan* with all its contents including the articles which had been used to prepare the corpse. Slowly Loco led the horse along the trail to the grave. The two sons-in-law lifted the light body to their shoulders, and with it followed the horse while Tuli brought up the rear. It was his duty to warn the chance traveler that this was the procession of death and he had better go by another route. In silence the party moved, careful not to speak or spit, lest one leave a trace of himself on that undesirable trail. Tuli, instead of following directly, moved in an arc so as to avoid as far as possible the path of the dead. They moved slowly, careful not to turn even a small pebble out of its position. If they had done so, sudden death would have befallen the offender unless he replaced it. The retinue stalked the dreadful trail so as to leave no trace of having covered it even as they would have done if pursued by the most terrible enemy.

Arrived beneath the crevice, the men deposited the body in it, unpacked the horse and laid the valuables neatly on top of the corpse. Then, as hastily as possible, they filled the fissure with rocks making it appear that they had always been there. Tuli led the horse directly under the grave and shot it between the eyes. There it was left with bridle, saddleblanket, saddle and cinch, just as it had been in life. The four mourners returned home, not sedately as they had come, but by hopping and skipping, careful to avoid brush and cactus and choosing a way different from that by

125

which they had come so that by the time they arrived home they had nearly described a circle.

While the burial was taking place Dezba, surrounded by the children and grandchildren who were home—even the herd-boy was among them for all activitiy had ceased—sat in her *hogan* looking at the floor. No one spoke, ate or drank. Not until after the pallbearers had returned and, by bathing and shampooing their hair, had removed the most imminent danger of contamination, could the family eat. For four days they sat quietly, eating little, doing no work, moving only when it was positively necessary. By standing with his back to the traveler and motioning with his hands over his shoulders, a man guarded the trail from the *hogan* to the grave, indicating to the intruder ignorant of the family's loss, that he was on the trail of the dead, and should turn aside. When four nights had passed in grieving, all the mourners purified themselves by bathing and once more took up their accustomed duties.

The four days of mourning were appropriate for visits of comfort, but the severity of the weather prevented many from even hearing of the chanter's death. Slowly, as the news spread and as the roads made it possible, friends and relatives came. They entered the *hogan* more reticently than usual. A woman went up to Dezba, hid her head on Dezba's shoulder and together they sobbed unrestrainedly. Since Dezba was the closest relative of the deceased, each woman "cried" longest with her, some for as long as twenty minutes. Meanwhile the companions of the woman were weeping in the same fashion with Dezba's daughters. Men who were closely related grieved together in the same way. More commonly though, they expressed their sorrow by a long-continued silent handclasp as their eyes filled with tears. The first time she saw them thereafter, even if it happened to be years later, Dezba would greet close relatives and friends by sobbing. Their comfort would lack nothing of formality or sincerity because chance caused its expression to be long delayed.

Lassos-a-warrior's kin had burned the *hogan* in which he died because the fearsome part of his spirit lingered about the place. It was not exactly his ghost for it had no form. It was called *chindi* and was perhaps not personal or something belonging especially to him, but rather the essence of contamination. It was harmful only if disturbed. *Some people deserted the place where one had died instead of burning it.* The family moved away and ever after such a *hogan* was given a wide berth by all Navajo.

There was no fear of the memory of Dezba's brother as there was of his dead body and the place where he died. Constantly his family referred to his ways and his acts, recalling them lovingly. Several weeks after his death Dezba and Silversmith began to discuss the question of moving. Although their establishment was large and seemingly permanent, they agreed that they would be happier elsewhere, for the house, the fire, the shade, the whole range seemed full of the vibrant spirit of the departed. In vain the survivors cocked their ears for the tramp of the wiry horse and the lilt of the piercing song. At best there was only the dreary whistle of the wind; worse was the silence which strained the ear beyond endurance.

It did not take Dezba's men long to build her a new *hogan* a quarter of a mile south of the old one. When hers was finished, they moved the logs of those belonging to her daughters and soon a new settlement had sprung up. The move eased the pain a little, for the beloved brother had no place in the new *hogan,* the horse had not been tethered habitually to the familiar cedar outside, the bridle had no accustomed nail.

· · · · · · · · ·

The soul of Lassos-a-warrior, "that which stood within him," was regarded as his life principle. He has not gone to some other world where he retains his individuality and conceits. He came from we know not where, from the Earth which is the source of all things. His life and his ideals were of the earth earthy. He lived them all in order that he might, while breathing, follow the beautiful trail to the harmony which is above all things. He cannot now be in another world for he has gone back to the earth from which he originated. Now he needs no song for, having lost his identity, he is a part of it all, an indefinable part, he is not only of it, he *is* it, the ultimate essence toward which man and all things earthly strive.

128

11

Groping

THE YEARNING for information and understanding which impelled John Silversmith to leave home for school even after his first discouraging experience never left him. A docile or phlegmatic pupil started his education at one school, and if he did not return home, continued as far as that school would take him. But John was neither phlegmatic nor docile. After three years at the school nearest his home, he made up his mind to try another and managed to get to it. Having arrived from a long distance, he was allowed to stay. His first move was typical of all his schooling. Everywhere he went, he was given different advice. Indian children were not compelled to go to school at all, or to a particular school, and the course John followed was far from systematic.

There was hardly an Indian boarding-school which he had not attended. He was always sure that the one he heard about would be more suitable for him than the one where he was. He was sometimes able, through his winning smile and amiable disposition, to effect a transferal. If he could not do so, he transfered himself. He simply left one school and turned up some days later at another. Distance was no barrier; it was in fact an advantage for he loved the excitement and unpredictability of travel. Furthermore, since he could never see a way to get back to where he came from, officers of the new school felt that since he had come so far they might as well give him a chance.

By the time he was twenty-one he had acquired a broad education and a wide range of interests all on a very shallow foundation. At this time the Soil Erosion Control division of the Department of Agriculture of the U.S. Government was seeking intelligent interpreters for training to carry out an ambitious plan of soil rehabilitation on the Navajo Reservation. In connection with this work John Silversmith wandered into the Hogan School which existed to teach Navajo interpreters to write their own language and to find the means for adult education in their own communities where the Department of Indian Affairs was about to open a number of new day-schools.

The school was held in a hogan during the summer months and consisted only of teacher and adult Navajo students with pencils, paper and a blackboard. The teacher told John Silversmith that its purpose was to deal with educational problems with equipment available to even the most isolated Navajo. The simplicity of the idea appealed to him and he attended faithfully for the month which was considered a session.

The experience of the other students in securing an education was as varied as John's. His own ramblings had convinced him that the education white people could give Navajo children would be more beneficial if they were not taken away from home. One of the students of the Hogan School had organized and conducted a day school successfully for two years before the Government undertook its more ambitious new plan. John Silversmith with the other students listened attentively and sympathetically to the story she told explaining why she had persisted in her work under the almost insurmountable difficulties which confronted her:

"When I was about eight—that would have been twenty-eight years ago—my father took me to Gallup to be sent to school with the other children. You know, of course, that those who gather up the children for school do not know the difference between Navajo and other Indian children, or at least they didn't then," she explained to the teacher. "I was put in with a bunch of Hopi children and sent to Santa Fe. I was so homesick I nearly died, but toward spring the other children began to look down the road hoping their parents would come to get them. Quite a good many came, but no one came for me. I do not think my parents even knew where I was. The next spring I again watched the clouds of dust and again no one came out of them. So I stayed four years and then a group of Hopi children was taken back by train. I was taken with them. I didn't know much, but I knew they would be taken to Winslow. I knew if I was put off the train there I wouldn't know what to do. I begged and begged the disciplinarian to let me off at Gallup, and finally he put me off the train and there I was alone. I thought I could find my father but the station Master would not let me go out into Gallup alone. He did not know where to go, even if he could have gone with me. I was sure I could find my father, if he would only let me go, but he wouldn't. I just stayed there and cried and cried. At last Mr. Hubbell, the one they called Don Lorenzo, came in. The Station Master told him of my trouble. He took me with him and luckily my father was in town and we found him. I was young then, but I remember it all as if it was yesterday, especially watching those hopeless clouds of dust. I made a vow that if ever I could do anything to keep a Navajo child from being taken from its parents I

131

would do it. That is why I am in favor of day schools and that is why I have struggled to show they can be a success, even if it was hard."

There had never been any doubt in the mind of this woman that Navajo children would come back to their homes to live. John Young, another student who had been fortunate enough to work at an agency after he left school, told why many educated Navajo did not want to live on the Reservation:

"I went to school when I was very young. When I went home, it seemed as if I didn't know how to talk to my father and the rest of my relatives. Not that I did not speak or understand Navajo, but because they knew nothing of the things in which I was interested. I was not interested in the things they talked about either. I thought they did not know anything. Now I realize that we 'did not talk the same language.' One time when I was about fourteen I went home for two weeks. I was so lonesome, I could think of nothing to do but to go out and hoe in the cornpatch. I hoed real *hard* for hours to keep from crying. I could never go back and live with my people. But I would like to help teach them the things we know, especially things about health and how to get a better living."

Another fellow-student was John Bigay who gave his reasons for attending the Hogan School as well as those for which the School existed. During his forty-five years of life he had interpreted for missionaries, artists, ethnologists and government officials. He was especially interested in law, had acted as court interpreter and was a judge.

"When a man makes a will, I want to be able to put down exactly what he says. I don't want to have to translate it into English so I can write it. Then it is only what I *think* he said. I can read and write Navajo in the various ways it has been written, but I want to get enough practise in one way to write it *fast*. This is the only way I have found which I can read without an English translation. It may be all right for other Indian tribes

132

to write only English, but they are not the same as the Navajo because more of their people know English and their population is small. Why! here even the traders and missionaries try to learn Navajo so they can understand our people."

John Tallman, another student, spoke for interpreters when he said,

"When we have to interpret speeches of the Government officials, even of the Commissioner himself, we have to do it in public on the spur of the moment. Just the other day I had to translate 'Trachoma is endemic and epidemic in the Navajo population.' I honestly don't know what that means. We all have different ways of translating such words as 'germs,' 'antiseptic,' 'trachoma,' and 'tuberculosis.' If we were able to read and write them, we could use the words more uniformly, and make our people understand them more easily and clearly. I think too the white people could learn to understand Navajo better if it was written."

As John Silversmith became acquainted with the other students at the Hogan School he realized that their interests were the same as his. He had arrived three days after the session had begun and the teacher gave him the alphabet which was being used. There were thirty-eight symbols, each illustrated by a simple Navajo word with its English equivalent. By the time John Silversmith came the students who had started on the first day were writing compositions. For two days he studied the symbols and made observations, but did not participate in the work of the class, or contribute a single remark. On the third day he was able to write Navajo with few errors and to correct the work of the others. This he did as if he had been writing Navajo all his life and was a recognized authority on the subject. The others accepted his criticism as a matter of fact, as indeed they did all corrections.

By the time Dezba's son was ready to write the class was working on a health talk. The teacher had asked the students to write about germs so as to explain to people who had never heard of their existence their action and danger, and ways to prevent disease from spreading. For half a day the pupils worked without producing a word. Always before they had written much, for they were fluent with ideas and with words to express them. The teacher found that their own understanding of the subject was vague. Nearly two days were spent discussing the subject.

During this time Shooting Chanter, an old Navajo medicine-man, came in to visit the School and the pupils explained their difficulties to him. He who acknowledged nothing new under the sun told them a Navajo story:

"In the old days the Navajo did not have the diseases which are prevalent to-day. The life they lived was hard, famine and drouth were ever-present threats. As time went on fawns became scarcer and scarcer. Even in those days the Navajo had sings, but all had not yet originated. The old men made up sings to cure new troubles. They decided to start a new one to increase the number of fawns. They spotted their bodies with white clay to make them look like fawns. They had masks and put them on while they sang. But when the singers took off the masks, they had sores wherever the clay had spotted them, and fawns were as scarce as ever. At that time they made a rule that no one should ever wear a mask unless he was in perfect health."

After the discussion, John Bigay wrote an introduction, John Tallman brought the subject up to date, and John Silversmith drew an illustration for the article. Since it was to be mimeographed, he made a stencil with a darning needle, and numerous copies of the explanation were made in Navajo and English.

"A hundred years ago our people lived so that they were able to endure many hardships, cold, for example, heat, hunger, thirst and poverty, and at that time they did not have much disease. Death did not take many

The precipitous walls of the canyon were a better protection than forts. →

because all were capable of withstanding much suffering. So it was that our (now) deceased grandmothers and grandfathers lived. Our old men tell us about it.

"About seventy-five years ago with the railroad the Whites came among us and seemed to pour into our midst all kinds of diseases: whooping-cough, rashes of all kinds, measles, and smallpox. Just as dangerous were what we call tuberculosis and eye troubles, especially the 'one which makes the eyelids rough' (trachoma).

"Now they are trying to prevent epidemics, that is, something of a special kind which causes sickness and seems to start without a cause. The sicknesses seem to come from certain so-called wormlike objects which we do not understand because we cannot see them. The white people under-stand something about them because they have a kind of glass called a microscope with which they can see these worm-things. They have no Navajo name and for that reason are not easy to explain precisely. These so-called germs seem to exist almost everywhere and perhaps they are not all harmful. Perhaps only those which start from our own bodies are the ones which give trouble, those in our saliva, in our blood, those on what we eat and drink from (our dishes), those in what we lie on (our bedding). We Navajo are generous with our possessions. We consider it stingy not to let our brother use the same cup and towel, but of course we never think about these worms since we are ignorant of their effects.

"It would be much better if we were careful not to transfer these worms which we cannot see. It may be true that facilities for washing are limited, but every day the sun traverses the sky. The doctors teach us that the sun can annihilate most of these germs. So if you would put your dishes, clothing, and bedding outside it would be a good thing, for the harmful worms would be tortured by his heat. As for us, we would all live more healthily."

135

They could call upon their gods at the White House . . . .

As the Hogan School continued it became clear that the students most needed education in subjects which were taught only in colleges and universities, although only two of them had the equivalent of a high school training and that was vocational, not academic. They wanted to know the origin and history of the Indians, and in this connection they were deeply interested in geography. Those who were working with the Soil Erosion project felt a need for information they could get only by a study of botany, forestry, agronomy, zoology, animal husbandry and geology. John Bigay had a consuming desire to read law. He had interpreted for an ethnologist who was studying genealogy and kinship terms and he wanted to know more about that, even as he desired to study linguistics. John Tallman had spent two years at the State University where he had had a course in archaeology and one in anthropology. John Silversmith was interested in all these subjects with wonderful high-sounding names and had read some books dealing with them. When he had graduated from the last vocational school he had attended, he had been advised to go to college.

Since the lives of the students were more nearly concerned with matters dealt with in ethnology, archaeology and linguistics, these subjects were taught at the Hogan School. The students were alike in their groping desire for greater learning, in their ignorance of the way to get it, and in their lack of preparatory background. Most of them could draw nicely, and two had real talent in art. Several were carpenters and two were expert mechanics. One had read a book on Einstein, another treasured a classical English grammar which he had read many times, and a third had studied with care every word of the Wheeler-Howard Reorganization Act about which the Navajo were much excited at the time.

The ability to concentrate was a second unifying trait of the diversified class. Many of them, like John Silversmith, started the course late, but once at the School nothing short of the exhaustion of a subject made them pause. Just as they talked for hours on end at Navajo council meetings and as they sang through the long hours of the night, so they applied themselves each day to the subject in hand. If there was one not satisfied with his understanding when school was dismissed he would continue his work on the subject until, by his own efforts, he had mastered his difficulties.

The teacher was often amused and surprised, sometimes even slightly shocked, at the way the students ridiculed one another. She was accustomed to teaching white students whom she had to correct gently lest they become insulted. To the Navajo there was no personal element in mistakes. They were errors, they must not stand, they might be pointed out in a jocular manner. Indeed, certain inaccuracies were greeted by a loud guffaw and might be followed up by quips and continued pointed references.

There are certain sounds in Navajo as in French which are called "nasalized" because they are sounded through the nose. John Silversmith pronounced this word several times as "nozzleized." The teacher corrected him and the class shouted with laughter, but John argued coolly, "Well! some people say 'can't' and others say 'cahn't.' Why can't this *a* be pronounced the same way?"

"Because this is not that kind of an *a* and besides, your pronunciation makes it sound like the end of a hose."

This pleased the class even more than John's lapse, and their mirth silenced, if it did not convince him. The next time the sign of nasalization was omitted, John Tallman said solemnly, "I think the *o* ought to be nosealized."

John Silversmith laughed with the rest and never again did he mispronounce the word.

A large portion of the time spent at the Hogan School was spent in discussing methods of education. For many years the Navajo had sent their children to boarding-school. There was now a movement afoot to establish day schools throughout the Navajo territory. The educational problems were difficult no matter what policy was advocated. For years the Navajo had resisted sending their children, especially the girls, away from home, for parents and children sometimes lost account of each other as was the case with the plucky little day school teacher. If parents knew where their children were, they nevertheless felt that the children were lost to their relatives and surroundings when they returned ill-adapted to the life they had to live as was Mary, the Twins' Mother, and many others. But now that a day school program was being worked out, many of the Navajo opposed it on the grounds that they themselves would have to supply food and clothing for their children, matters which the Government took care of at the boarding-schools. The students of the Hogan School thought that parents ought to maintain their children and that opposition from this source could be overcome by persuasion, especially since a hearty dinner was to be furnished by the school at noon.

Much more difficult was the problem of distance. Some of the Navajo families thought they were crowded if they had neighbors within a radius of four miles. Furthermore, they were used to changing their abode when circumstances demanded or when whim dictated. Seasons caused such changes, not only in the yearly cycle, but also according to the amount of rainfall at any time. John Silversmith explained the obstacles confronting the establishment of day schools encountered by those working at Soil Erosion Control:

"One of the objectives of the Government is to get the Navajo to settle down into more permanent groups. This they are trying to do by putting more land under cultivation through irrigation development. The theory is that more people can live on the same amount of land if they carry on more agriculture than they can by herding large flocks of sheep. This is of course apparent and it has been proved in the Shiprock region where many acres have been farmed for a long time with water from the San Juan. But it will mean a basic change in the entire Navajo economy if it is extended all over the Reservation. The Navajo are putting up a very strong resistance to the plan because they do not want to be tied down to a small area. They want to wander about as they do now. Besides, they do not think there is enough water available at many places on their 16,000,000 acres for such elaborate irrigation projects to keep them all. And some say too, that after the white man gets the Navajo country all nicely fixed up so that the land is valuable, they will chase the Navajo off of it. We are up against all these things in trying to teach them to conserve the soil.

"What is more we want to start the schools now. Since the Navajo do not yet have land to till, they have to live on their sheep. The number of sheep they can pasture near a day school is much restricted if we get them to agree to range control as they have done at some places."

"That is putting a lot in a nutshell," said John Tallman, "and there is another kind of trouble. At Chinlee the people have always carried on agriculture, even without irrigation. But there isn't a single road around there good enough for a bus to travel so the children would have to walk awful far to go to school. Another objection put up by the old people is that the buses are dangerous and they would not like to have their children travel in them."

As the discussion continued the students agreed that all these difficulties must be met by persuasion and successful demonstration. The day school teacher had a suggestion, "We have all of those problems at Red House too. When I started the school there people said we couldn't do it. But I went and talked to some of the families and they coöperated by sending their children. Some who came at the very first lived far away and had to walk. But they liked to come, they told others, and now we have an average attendance of thirty although two years ago we started with only ten. Now we have a bus and they are not afraid of it, and we have never had any accidents. These people have only their small cornpatches and herd sheep most of the time. Because they come and see the school at work and because the children talk about it favorably, we keep getting more pupils. Now the Government promises us a building. We have been holding school in the 'chapter house' so far. The Government did put water in for us."

"What Mrs. Curly says is right," said John Young. "Lots of times when you can't tell our people anything you can show them. The old men do not like to be told what to do by the young ones. People at the Agency always blame us for not going back and teaching our people what we have learned at school. They do not understand that our elders tell us what to do, they do not ask us. Once in a while we might make a suggestion but if it is not taken up we cannot do anything more. If we insisted, we would seem disrespectful. Returned students often make that mistake, but it doesn't get them anywhere. I have often noticed that returned students are impatient and in a hurry when talking to the old men. The old men then become stubborn and nothing can budge them. If the Government would give us someone to show us how to conduct the community centers, I am sure we could bring about great changes, but they would have to come slowly. And showing the people would do more good than talking to them."

140

12

Heir

JOHN SILVERSMITH went to his state university the fall after he attended the Hogan School, and the teacher whom the Navajo called Red Woman, did not see him for two years. When she met him again he told her he had been studying hard. He had taken courses in geology, archaeology and anthropology. His favorite subject was philosophy, but he wanted to work intensively on Indian languages. From the time he had attended the Hogan School he had been writing Navajo, and by reading, he had learned much of the theory of recording unwritten languages. He had become so ambitious that he had started to write a Navajo grammar. Since there was instruction only in modern written languages at John's university, he thought it would be best for him to transfer to a university where Indian languages were taught.

From the authorities of the University Red Woman learned that John, when only a freshman, had chosen upper-class subjects. He had been told that he must take certain courses to give him preparatory credits, and had taken these demands as lightly as usual. He had taken a beginning language, in which he had not done very well in spite of his linguistic ability. He had failed in College Algebra. He had had a course in English composition, yet his English, though fluent, left much to be desired. His two year record showed that he had done well in the subjects which interested him but had failed to fulfil requirements.

As they settled down for a long talk, Red Woman asked John, "Why do you try to get a degree when it means such a long hard struggle?"

"There is a rule of the Department of Indian Affairs that no one can get an appointment as a teacher without a normal school certificate or a college degree. I think I could teach my people. I would like to live somewhere on the Reservation where I could show the grownups some of the things I have learned. I am sure I could convince them that the practice of white medicine is really curative, while sings are not only not effective, but often harmful. I would like to teach young people that, even if they live on the Reservation, as they must, they can enjoy a great deal of the learning that white people have.

"There are many things I would like to do that I think I can do. I think that the Navajo social system works better than the system you have. But I don't think the white people understand it, and I should like to investigate it and write it up so they would. And then there is the religion! There is so much I want to do about that! I want to get the ideas of the old men down in their own words, and show what they really think, for their religion is not nonsense. It contains all their artistic life, art, music, poetry. I would like to have a chance to do Navajo ethnology."

"To do that you have to be attached to an institution interested in the subject," suggested Red Woman. "To learn how to do it you have to have special training and you can't get that without a degree, for it is all gradu-

There was a mellow simplicity with a strong touch of humor and ....forbearance .... →

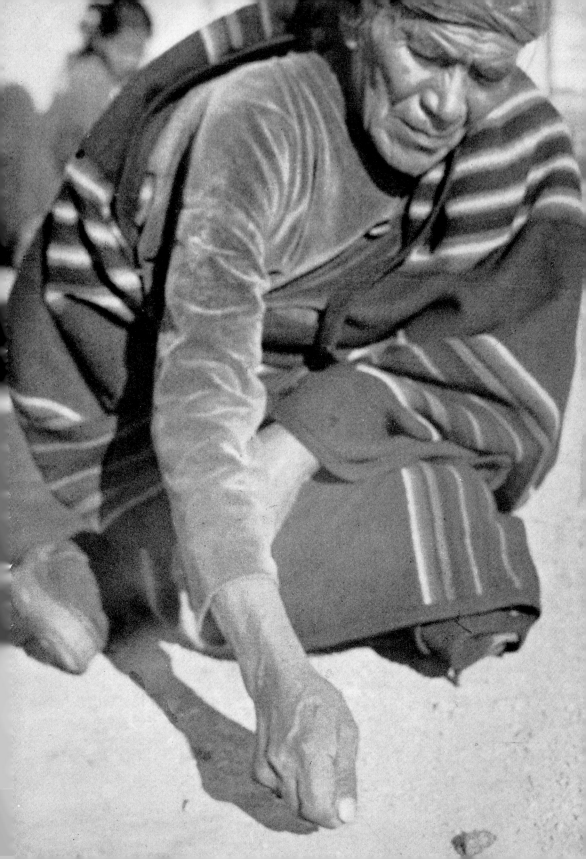

The sheep were fat, the wool was thick and sleek . . . .

Some people deserted the place where one had died instead of burning it.

ate work. Why is it you are not working off your requirements? You have not taken the courses which the Registrar required, and you have not done well enough in others. From the way you talk to me I cannot believe you are not able to pass. And Professor X tells me you do his work well."

"When I work with you, I am doing what I want to do most, and that is true also of philosophy which Professor X teaches. There are two reasons why I don't do the other things well. The first is that I am not interested in the subjects that are required. And the second is that I am not prepared to take them. Maybe I would like them if I had the preparation. I sit in classes with students who have gone to high school and have spent at least four years of their life studying to get ready for college. And what have I been doing? I have been at school longer than they have, but you can't expect to be ready for college with preparation at vocational schools. I have been washing dishes, making beds, working in the laundry, driving a bus! Oh yes, we draw and paint and carve and weave, but those things don't help you at college.

"Why, I can't even get the reading done. That is because I never learned to read properly. Long ago someone told me to look up every word I didn't know in the dictionary. There are a great many I don't know, so I start to look up words and then I forget what I am doing and find myself reading the dictionary. That's why it takes me so long to do assigned reading."

"What was the matter with mathematics?" asked Red Woman. "There are many white people who say that Indians cannot learn it. Do you believe that?"

At this John laughed ruefully, "Of course I don't believe it," and he got up and began to stalk up and down the room as he talked. "It all goes back to the same cause. I was taking College Algebra and I never had seen an algebra book before. They don't teach things like that in vocational schools. I am sure I could have passed it if I had had beginning Algebra. I bought an elementary book and tried to make it up, but it was too much. I couldn't keep up with the class. The professor told me that if he explained all I needed to know he would not have time to teach the rest of his class."

"Did you like it?" asked Red Woman.

"Well, I didn't understand enough to know whether I did or not. But I am sure if I could do it from the beginning, I would like it. Of course Indians can do mathematics if they are taught. I know an Indian from Nevada who is majoring in it and his professors say he is very good. He gets good marks in it. Then there is another thing. I don't see that I need it much. So when I had got in so deep I couldn't see my way out, I just quit and spent the time on things I thought I could use."

"Was English one of those?"

"Yes, I spent an awful lot of time on English. One of the teachers gave me hours of tutoring, and yet I did not get a very good mark. If there were rules I could learn, it would be easier. But it seems every time I get something straight there is an exception the next time I use it. For instance, the English teacher said I should never use the article 'a' before a plural. Then I used 'few people' in the next sentence, and she said it ought to be 'a few people.' I thought both 'few' and 'people' were plural and cannot see why one should say 'a few people' if the rule is any good."

Red Woman sympathized with the English teacher and with John, as he continued, "I can't learn which nouns are singular and plural in English because their meanings are so different from Navajo. For instance, when we speak of firewood we think of each stick separately, and I reason that ought to be 'woods' in English, but of course it isn't. Some of these things I know, but I have no feeling for singulars, plurals, and collectives when I want to use expressions which no one has discussed with me. Do you have to learn every expression separately? That is very hard. I really tried to do well in English, but I am never sure of anything."

"Now you know how helpless I sometimes feel about learning Navajo," laughed Red Woman. "There must be rules in Navajo, but everything seems like an exception to me," and she went back to his aspirations for teaching his people. "If you had a chance to work with your people, what would you do first?" she asked.

"The first thing I would do would be to work with the medicine-men to try to get them to give up some of the harmful things they do, and adopt certain medical principles," said John.

"Do you think there is any possibility of changing them?" asked Red Woman.

"Yes," said John. "I know there is. I know a chanter who has thought a great deal about the number of deaths from pneumonia. He has talked to educated fellows a lot and they have convinced him that the bathing and shampooing and wakefulness of a long sing are too hard on the patient. He does not make the patient move about as much as the sing requires. When it is time for the bath, he sees to it that there is a good fire, and that the water is warm. He sees to it too that there is no draft, and that the patient does not go outside until after the hair is dry. He has someone else go outside instead. If the lungs seem bad with pleurisy the singer may have the patient lie wrapped in his blanket resting during the entire sing. And when it is over he makes very sick patients rest."

"How does he explain away the necessity for endurance and wakefulness?" asked Red Woman.

"He makes the patient do all of that sometime after he gets well. This singer told me that he had more cures since he did this. I believe one could teach them about germs too," continued John. "I would not do as others who have become Christians have done, tell them that everything they do is wrong and they ought to cut out all the sings. The Navajo believe in them and get a great deal of comfort and pleasure out of them.

If I had a chance, I would not be in a hurry to change. Changes would have to be a slow growth. One has to be patient and do a lot of talking and work things out gradually.

"There is another difficulty you run into in talking with the old men and that is, everything you tell them that science has worked out they already know. You remember that when we were writing about germs Shooting Chanter told us a story and said that the ancient singers made a rule that nobody who was not in perfect health could wear a mask. Of course the trouble is in determining who is in perfect health. I always think trachoma can be spread rapidly by the masks. One would have to explain and show the singers how it spreads, but you can't do it by making them give up everything they think is important.

"Once I was telling my uncle about dinosaurs and the big animals that used to inhabit the earth in prehistoric times. And he said he knew all about them. They were the monsters of Navajo legend which were killed by Enemy Slayer. Their bones can still be seen turned to rock like Shiprock. Nothing is new to the old men who know the traditions."

"Do you have any answer for the medicine-men who complain about those who die at the hospital, or under a doctor's care?"

"I keep telling them that the reason is that the sick were taken too late. It is hard to show them that doctors can do most good when an illness is just beginning. The Navajo cannot understand that, after sickness had progressed, it is hard or even impossible to cure, whereas it might be easily curable at the beginning. They usually do not notice first symptoms at all. Then of course I tell them that their cases do not always get cured either."

"But don't they tell you of many cures from the sings?" asked Red Woman.

"Oh yes," laughed John. "And I must say they have a good many fine

146

arguments compared to the number of those cured at the hospital. Of course they never consider that most cases are nearly dead before they are taken to the hospital. I used to have lots of discussions with my uncle about them. He told of a great many successes at singing which I could not explain, cures which seemed miraculous. And I know of some myself.

"There was a boy at school called Chiki. He had frequent severe hemorrhages, and the school doctor said he could do nothing for him, and sent him home to die. His grandfather sang an Apache Wind Chant over him and he got well. I know that boy and saw him when he was ill. At another time he was completely helpless with rheumatism and said his arms and legs burned. He had consulted two white doctors and neither of them helped him. Then he had the Shooting Chant sung over him, and he is now fat and healthy.

"Another hopeless case was that of a Bead Chanter. He had become ill and for years grew steadily worse. Finally his white friends prevailed upon him to go to a hospital. The doctor there said he had cancer of the stomach and sent the old man home to die. He had sixty-five miles to go and had to stop with relatives three times on the way, taking altogether five weeks to get there. When he arrived home he had the Evil Chasing Big Star Chant sung over him. For many years he had not sung himself, although he had been one of the most powerful chanters in his neighborhood. Today he is singing again, and he has even undertaken to learn a new chant. His illness had made him old. The chant literally restored him to youth, as the prayers say. When I talk to the old men I cannot give any explanation of cases like these and I do not try to. I can only try to influence them to try the hospital when I see someone is ill."

"I have been puzzled as much myself," said Red Woman. "Our friend, the trader, told me of an exceptional case which I can hardly believe and yet all the evidence is vouched for by the white people who were concerned

with the case. A delegation of Navajo came to Always-in-a-hurry one afternoon and told him that Little Singer's wife had had a baby at the hospital.
She had contracted an infection and was going to die. The trader knew
that what they said was true for the doctor had told him only a few hours
before that there was no hope for the woman. Knowing both sides of the
case and having great regard for Little Singer and his faith, Always-in-a-
hurry found it hard to give the only advice he thought possible. Nevertheless he told the Navajo they could not take the woman away. 'If you
let her go to the hospital,' he said, 'you must let the doctor have full
charge.'

"After dark the leaders of the party, much frightened, came back to the
trader. They had insisted in spite of his advice on taking the woman from
the hospital. Naturally the doctor had become very angry. As they carried
her out of the door, she fainted or went into a coma. As the Navajo say,
she died. Then they wanted to take her back, but the doctor said, 'Indeed
not! You insisted on taking her, now you have to keep on with it.'

"The woman's relatives then took her to the *hogan* they had prepared
for the sing and she came to. They had come to the trader to get supplies
for the ceremony. They told him they had a douche bag made of kidskin
with a bone tube. A man had been sent a long distance to get a plant from
which they were going to make a medicine for syringing. The trader was
desperate and gave them some Dakin's solution. He thought of telling me
this story because the woman who 'died' as she was removed from the hospital was at the trading-post at the time. With her were three young children, the one born at the time and two born since.

"I wouldn't say that Always-in-a-hurry believes in the Navajo ways altogether, but he thinks there is something we cannot explain. And when
he asks me to account for cases like these, I feel like you do in trying to
convert the old men to scientific medicine. I think though that you, with

patience and sympathy for their beliefs, ought to get somewhere with it. No one can do it who does not know what life is like in a Navajo *hogan* and I believe you could succeed if you had time enough."

"Well, I would like to try," said John optimistically. "I think I have done some good already, and I can't expect to do it all at once. I don't have any comeback for examples such as we have mentioned, but there are many cases of persons who die and I know they could have been saved. Those are telling cases although I only believe, I cannot prove, they would have been saved. The mortality among Navajo from puerperal fever used to be fierce. Now since women go to the hospital, the fatalities are few, and yet my uncle used to tell of a single case like the one you mentioned, and you would think that none of the Navajo ever died of the same disease.

"But when I consider the strength of their faith, and their ignorance of scientific progress," continued John, "I can understand the reasoning of the medicine-men. It is when fellows like my cousin who was brought up like a white child, go back into the mountains to be sung over, that I become discouraged about it all. One day Lassos-a-warrior asked me why he had done it, if the white man's medicine is so good. What would you have told him?"

Red Woman well knew that John's cousin had for years been away from the Navajo studying at white schools. He had gone so far as to secure a professional degree. Recently he had come back to do social work among his people with whom his contacts had been few and tenuous. As she thought over John's remark, Red Woman wondered if the cousin had had the sing believing his work would become more successful, but she could only answer, "I don't know. I don't think I could have given your uncle a convincing answer."

149

13

Visiting

IT IS NEARLY TWO YEARS since Dezba established her camp at the sheepdip, more than four since her John attended the Hogan School. The sun, benignly giving place to a bright moon, casts its long winter rays over the closely set trees which surround a clearing. For less than fifteen minutes, eerie in their beauty, it transforms mangy dogs to saints by limning them in gold. It presents a furry halo to the discouraged horses, munching away at their cornhusk supper. As the glory subsides it weakens on huge stacks of wood and catches a parting glint from the glistening hair of the woodchoppers or from one of the axes they wield. At the east blue mass chases a pink edge from horizon to zenith where blue and pink merge into darkness. Dogs, horses and woodchoppers soon become indistinct bulks casting shadows in the silver path of the moon.

For the nine days during which the night chant has been held on the well-wooded mountain side, the hosts and their guests, who are their helpers as well, have been hauling dry cedar and pinyon and chopping it into lengths which can be carried. It is all to be burned this night as the large audience keeps chilly vigil until the freezing dawn. In front of the ceremonial hogan a wide space has been set off by a fence of fires along each side.

As the shadows lengthen Tuli helps Silversmith remove the seat from the new wagon of which they are very proud. They place it as near as possible to the third fire from the hogan on the south side. They know that this will be the front row of the audience, the most advantageous point for seeing the dances. A somewhat low wind blows from the south and although the onlookers must expect some smoke in their eyes from the many fires behind Dezba's family, there will be less on the south side of the dance place. On the wagon seat Tuli arranges blankets and heavy comforts with care. In carrying wood for the fire they are aided by Loco and Gray Girl's new husband, who after arranging all the heavy things in order for the women, leave so that their mother-in-law may take possession.

Now that a new camp has been made ready, Dezba's family move from the wagon near which they had camped all day. Gray Girl is there and Loco's wife with her five children, for Alaba has a new baby brother. Little Policeman is with them of course and all are happy to have his mother with them for she has returned from the hospital. By placing the wagonseat Tuli has reserved the place for the night's camp. Everybody helps to move the extra blankets and the boxes containing food, so their belongings will be safe and so that other families will not crowd in too close to them. After the bulky objects are moved, one member of the family or another keeps an eye on the new camp as the others make repeated and frequently interrupted trips from the old fire near the wagon, now reduced to coals, to the new one blazing its pointed way through dry cedar logs.

152

Even Lassos-a-warrior is here, for Dezba, carrying a Dutch oven and water-jug, is stopped on her way by an old woman come to greet her with tears because this is their first meeting since the death of Dezba's brother. At last all the belongings are stowed so they can be watched or used and the party circle changes frequently, growing larger or smaller as the evening progresses.

An hour after dark, Always-in-a-hurry moves along the space between the two straight lines of fires. His progress is slow for Navajo from all sides come out to greet him. At last he passes Dezba's camp. As he does so Tuli walks out to him with extended hand and Always-in-a-hurry comes up to Dezba's fire. He does not sit down, but when Dezba, "his mother," offers him coffee, he says, "This looks like a pretty good place. I have a party at the other end of the line, but we can't see very well there. I am going to bring them all down here. Red Woman is with us and some people you don't know. We'll have coffee when we get settled."

Much pleased, Dezba's relatives squeeze closer together; she throws down some more sheepskins and Tuli goes with the trader to help carry the blanketrolls. After some time Tuli returns and with him Red Woman and two other white people. Always-in-a-hurry will not be here for a while because his reception continues. He has to listen to Tall Curly's tale of woe—his wife is ill, a coyote killed seven of his sheep, he has no reliable herder, he cannot pay his bill, but would like some more flour.

John Bigay appears, they start to talk politics and others join the two until a circle forms. Only after much talk does Always-in-a-hurry remember he is moving his camp.

Meanwhile Red Woman has settled herself and the visitors. Always-in-a-hurry has asked Dezba to broil mutton ribs for him but he has not yet brought them. Coffee is ready and waiting. Dezba's family has had supper. As they wait Red Woman picks up the thread of events where she left

153

it two years before. She learns that Gray Girl was married last summer and expects a baby in June. Her husband is "back there somewhere," says Tuli, pursing his lips toward an indefinite place behind Dezba.

"Did Little Policeman ever get anything for his cow?" asks Red Woman.

"Oh yes. After about a year he got twenty dollars," says Tuli. "We don't have Yellow Mexican any more. I traded him for another horse which Little Policeman calls 'Questionmark' because he has a white mark like a backward turned questionmark on his face."

"I suppose Little Policeman goes to day school then," says Red Woman.

"Yes," replies Tuli. "He has gone for two years."

"How is he doing?"

"Fine! He is in the third grade. He can read and write. One day we had gone away and he was coming to meet us with his little wagon. When he got to the tall cedar on the road we were coming along the herdboy met him and asked him to help with the sheep. So he left his wagon and wrote in the dirt, 'Take this wagon home for me,' so we did when we got there."

"Does he like school?"

"Oh yes! We wanted to come here yesterday and bring him, but he wouldn't because of school. So we had to wait until today because it is Saturday. He will never go to a sing if he has to miss school. If there is no other way he will walk the six miles to school on Monday morning."

"What does he do during the week?" asks Red Woman.

"He and his uncle stay at our *hogan* near the alfalfa fields. That way he has only a mile and a half to walk every day."

"Can they cook?"

"Yes," says Dezba, smiling, "last week Little Policeman was complaining about our food and said he could cook it better."

"Why didn't you tell him to do your cooking?" laughs Red Woman. "How are your sheep?"

154

"We don't have very many this year," answers Dezba. "After the Government reduction there was a dry spell and we lost a lot, and then there was the big snow. We did not lose any ourselves because Tuli plowed a space where we kept them, but we had to give away a lot because our relatives needed them. This year the coyotes are bad. They go right into the corrals and take fullgrown goats. We don't have as much meat as we'd like this year. In the last two weeks we had to give up four head because people asked us to help with their sings. One was for this one."

"How many did you have when you dipped?" asks Red Woman.

"They didn't make us dip this year. They said the sheep were all right."

"Isn't that wonderful!" says Red Woman. "Four years ago you had to dip twice in the same summer."

On her way to Dezba's camp someone had called "Hello!" to Red Woman. She did not at once recognize Mary, the mother of the twins, who was only the wraith of her former self. When Red Woman asked her how she was, remarking on her thinness, Mary replied, "I have been in the hospital for four months." In her arms she clasped a sickly baby, its eyes obviously infected with trachoma. Although her husband seemed fat and good-natured, there was an air of oppressive dejection about Mary's camp which Red Woman could not shake off. "Mary has certainly gone back to the blanket," she thought as she moved on.

Now in talking to Dezba, Red Woman asks about Mary. "I never see her now," explains Dezba. "Her father-in-law kept coaxing his son until they went over to his place to live, and it is so far they don't get back often. One of her twins died. The other is not well. She was at the hospital, but she is all right now. She is soon going to have another baby."

"And how is Mrs. Whitehouse getting along?" inquires Red Woman.

"All right," answers Tuli, "but the son who came home to help her died last fall. She is having a hard time, but she is all right."

As item by item they bring the news up to date Always-in-a-hurry at last arrives. Under one arm he squeezes a sack containing fresh mutton, and loaves of bread threaten to fall from his arms at any moment. "Are you hungry?" he asks his guests, and as they admit they are, he says to Dezba, "Roast it as soon as you can, my mother. We are all starving." Dezba, with raised hand shielding her eyes from the flames, expertly scrapes glowing coals from the fire under the grill which has been awaiting her "son." She continues her talk with Red Woman as she watches the meat.

Engrossed in their talk, they have to be silenced by Always-in-a-hurry who tells Red Woman to be quiet, and whispers to the strangers, "Those dancers represent the gods. The man who stands before them with the basket is the singer of this chant and he is praying for the patient who stands beside him. Now the patient goes down the line of gods to sprinkle them with cornmeal for that is an offering and a prayer at the same time."

All is silent until the prayer is over and not until the masked dancers have retired from the plaza is the talk resumed. By this time the meat is broiled and the white people eat ravenously. Meanwhile Always-in-a-hurry explains to them the reasons for the ceremony and the rites of the eight days which preceded this last night.

As they eat and talk, they see Mary moving through the firelight. She is followed by her husband who is lugging the carcass of a sheep. Without words or explanation he gives the meat to Tuli, as Mary talks to Dezba and Always-in-a-hurry, almost ignoring Tuli. They all know that this is the first chance Mary has had to show her gratitude to Tuli for making the cradle boards for her babies, and her husband includes his thanks by making the presentation. Tuli, much pleased, accepts the gift but no one indicates the least surprise.

Always-in-a-hurry announces that John Silversmith is here, and after

156

some hours John seeks out his mother's camp. He has driven a carload of Whites from the University and as he has walked through the crowd has been detained by talk with other people. Now seeing the large jolly party around Dezba's fire, he adds his guests to their number. Always-in-a-hurry obligingly spreads out another blanket and all shift into smaller folds as they make room for the newcomers. Whites talk to Whites and for a few moments John and Red Woman seem alone in the crowd. She learns that he will get his bachelor's degree from the University in the spring, that he has recorded many songs and legends on phonograph records and that he is busy transcribing them in his spare moments.

"Did you get a scholarship from the Government this year?" she asks.

"No, they said that I could not get one because the Navajo had not voted to accept the Wheeler-Howard Act. I don't know what that has to do with it, but I had to borrow the money I need," says John as they are interrupted by the white strangers asking about the sing. "How much does it cost?" they ask. "They have to pay the singer and all who help him," answers John, "and they have to feed all the people who want to eat at the cookshade. It amounts to quite a lot."

"Why do they do it then, for I hear on all sides complaints that the Navajo are so poor this winter?" asks one of the guests.

"They are," answers Red Woman, "but they think having these sings will make things better. Dezba was just telling me they do not have as much meat as they want this winter. Her family has all the resources possible to a Navajo. They have a comparatively large flock, they have a garden, the men raise alfalfa, they have their quota of sheep in the demonstration area supervised by Soil Conservation Control, and the men work for wages. If things are skimpy with them, how must they be for people who depend only upon their sheep? But the Navajo are much like white people who complain most of their poverty after they have bought a new car or a fur coat. They will have a big sing, their friends will help them, and afterward they may be poor, but they are satisfied that they have done what is expected of them."

Turning back to John Red Woman asks, "What are you going to do when you finish college?"

"I have no idea," replies John cheerfully. "There are many things I would like to do but so far I can find no money for them. Perhaps I will try to go back to work for Soil Conservation Control."

At last all have finished their supper, and after more talk with Dezba and more explanations to the white guests, Red Woman says, "I am getting stiff. I am going to walk around and see who's here."

She starts off with one of the trader's guests and soon meets John Bigay who stands in a bevy of big-hatted Indians still talking on his favorite subject, politics. They all shake hands and after Red Woman introduces the white woman they go on.

They come to a large group of white people and in their midst sits John Tallman.

"Hello! John, how are you?" asks Red Woman.

"Fine!" he answers. "I am really in jail but they let me out to drive these people to the sing." Turning to the people with him he introduces Red Woman to a number of day school employees.

For a long time Red Woman stands talking and finally settles with the party for a talk. "I used to know Mrs. Curly. I always admired her greatly for the way she started that day school and the success she made of it. I heard she had to give up teaching because of her health. I never understood how she kept up as long as she did."

"She died last week," says John Tallman.

For a moment there is silence, then he continues, "Miss Richards there behind you is one of the teachers at Red House her old school."

158

"I hear you have a building now. Mrs. Curly was looking forward with much enthusiasm to its completion."

"Yes," answered Miss Richards, "it is a two-room school now. We have over seventy pupils. Mrs. Curly never had a chance to teach there because of her illness, but she kept right on helping us even after she gave up her work."

"We have a fine baby clinic," volunteers another woman who is the nurse at a dispensary run in connection with a day school twenty-five miles away. "Without Mrs. Curly I could never have started it. We all miss her terribly, but her work will go on."

"I don't see where you could possibly get seventy children around Red House," remarks Red Woman.

"We have a bus that makes two trips a day, covering twenty miles, and we have quite a number of children who walk two miles to the bus. One little boy walks more than three miles from where his family is living now," explains Miss Richards.

"They must like the school then," concludes Red Woman. "I know very well the Navajo wouldn't do that unless they wanted to. I always say they will do anything they really want to do and this proves my point."

"How it is with the other schools? Do they have good attendance?" asks Red Woman.

One of the party is a doctor who makes trachoma inspections at various day schools. "I know one school where the teacher has to go out and get the three pupils every day they come. Sometimes she can't find them. There is another which has only five pupils and they do not come regularly. But another one very far from civilization has thirty pupils. The teacher explained the Thanksgiving vacation to them. She said, 'Tomorrow you do not come to school, or the next day, the next or the next. After five nights you come back to school again.' Then a little nine-year-old girl, the brightest in the school, said glumly, 'No good!' At this school some of the children who do not live very far come on Saturday and Sundays to 'visit.' There is a great difference as you go from one school to another. Attendance depends on the season, on the district, and especially on the school."

"Is attendance higher or lower in all of the forty-seven day schools than it was the year they were opened?" asks Red Woman.

Another woman in the party is a supervisor and she says, "We keep a graph of weekly attendance in the office, and this week it has been the highest of any time since the day schools were established. We had an average of nearly seventeen hundred. From now on for two months or so the Navajo will be more settled for the winter, except of course for sings. This year the season was not hopelessly dry so they did not move to the mountain, but there was a good pinyon crop near Flagstaff and none here, so many families took their children there for a month or longer. Now most of them have come back. This habit of moving around makes our work awfully hard."

"I heard there was a lot of opposition when the Government stopped furnishing clothes to the children. What happened? Did the Government change the order?" asked Red Woman.

"No, it made our average attendance low last year, but the parents are getting over it now except in certain very conservative districts and in one where there is a lot of general opposition to the day schools. But in that district we can never do anything that suits the leader who is a great orator and he keeps them continually stirred up."

"Come see us when school is in session," urges Miss Richards. "and us . . . ," the nurse starts to say when Red Woman feels a nudge from behind her. She turns to see John Bigay perched upon a canteen, listening to the whole conversation.

John asks her a question. She moves about to answer and in so doing cuts off the attention of the Whites for a moment. She takes this opportunity to ask John about the matters uppermost in his mind at a time like this. "How is the liquor situation, John? Do you have much trouble?"

"Not tonight we don't," answers John. "That is because this sing is far away from everything and because it is so cold. But no matter what we do, there is always some liquor smuggled in around the edges. Of course it is much worse at a Squaw Dance than at a Night Chant. We can never get the fellows who are at the bottom of the smuggling."

"Why did John Tallman say he was in jail?" whispers Red Woman.

"He got six months for drinking. As you know he is one of our best men, but the drink gets them all, and this is his fourth offense this year. They let him out for this trip because there was no one else to drive this party and the Superintendent had orders from Washington to bring one of the women who is an investigator to this sing, so the rest came along . . ."

In the midst of her talk with John Bigay, John Silversmith appears. "Always-in-a-hurry sent me to tell you he is ready to go."

The two discover that the hour is something past midnight, and as they join their own party which is preparing to leave for home, they see that many of the audience have succumbed to the biting air, the pinyon smoke, the lulling cadence of the dancers before them, and lie huddled in their blankets totally oblivious of their surroundings. Fires are now huge heaps of glowing coals. Tuli has laid two logs on Dezba's fire and allows himself a final toast beside the flame before going to don his scanty costume so that he may join the dance. Dezba's family lie comfortably curled in sleep. But as Red Woman, following Always-in-a-hurry's party down the dance plaza, glances back, she sees Dezba sitting erect, her blanket pulled up to her eyes, keeping vigil in the firelight.

161